KT-526-206

SOFTWARE PROJECT SURVIVAL GUIDE

BY

PARK CAMPUS
LEARNING CENTRE
C & G C.H.E. P.O. Box 220
The Park
Cheltenham GL50 2QF
Tel: (0242) 532721

STEVE MCCONNELL

Microsoft Press

Software Project Survival Guide

Published by Microsoft Press
A Division of Microsoft Corporation
One Microsoft Way
Redmond, Washington 98052-6399

Copyright © 1998 by Steve McConnell

All rights reserved. No part of the contents of this book may be reproduced or transmitted in any form or by any means without the written permission of the publisher.

Library of Congress Cataloging-in-Publication Data
McConnell, Steve.
    Software Project Survival Guide : how to be sure your first important project isn't your last / Steve McConnell.
        p.   cm.
    Includes index.
    ISBN 1-57231-621-7
    1. Computer software--Development--Management.   I. Title.
QA76.76.D47M394 1997
005.1'068'4--dc21   97-37923
                                               CIP

Printed and bound in the United States of America.

 2 3 4 5 6 7 8 9   QMQM   2 1 0 9 8 7

Distributed to the book trade in Canada by Macmillan of Canada, a division of Canada Publishing Corporation.

A CIP catalogue record for this book is available from the British Library.

Microsoft Press books are available through booksellers and distributors worldwide. For further information about international editions, contact your local Microsoft Corporation office. Or contact Microsoft Press International directly at fax (425) 936-7329. Visit our Web site at mspress.microsoft.com.

Microsoft, Microsoft Press, Visual Basic, Visual C++, Windows, and Windows NT are registered trademarks of Microsoft Corporation. Java is a trademark of Sun Microsystems, Inc. Other product and company names mentioned herein may be the trademarks of their respective owners.

Frontispiece from WINNIE-THE-POOH by A.A. Milne, illustrated by E.H. Shepard. Copyright 1926 by E.P. Dutton, renewed 1954 by A.A. Milne. Used by permission of Dutton Children's Books, a division of Penguin Books USA Inc.

Acquisitions Editor: David Clark
Project Editor: Victoria Thulman

CONTENTS

Acknowledgments

As an experiment, I posted draft chapters of this book on my Internet Web site and invited readers to comment on them. Many people downloaded the chapters, and they contributed literally thousands of insightful review comments. The diversity of viewpoints was tremendous (bordering on overwhelming), and the book is more readable, cohesive, practical, and useful as a result.

Thanks first to the people who reviewed the whole manuscript. These people include Robert C. Burns (The Boeing Company), Lawrence Casey, Alan Brice Corwin (Process Builder), Thomas Duff, Mike Cargal, Pat Forman (Lynden), Manny Gatlin, Marc Gunter, Tom Hill, William Horn, Greg Hitchcock, Grant McLaughlin, Mike Morton, Matt Peloquin, David Roe, Steve Rinn, André Sintzoff, Matthew J. Slattery, and Beth Weiss.

I am also grateful to the people who commented on significant sections of the book, including Ray Bernard (Ray Bernard Consulting and Design), Steven Black, Robert Brown, Jacob L. Cybulski, Tom Gilb, Dick Holland, Gerard Kilgallon, Art Kilner, Steve Kobb, Robert E. Lee, Pete Magsig, Hank Meuret (Meuret Consulting), Al Noel, Karsten M. Self, Rob Thomsett, and Gregory V. Wilson.

Other people commented on one or more details of the manuscript, and I've listed those people where appropriate in the "Notes" section at the end of the book.

It was a pleasure to see the staff at Microsoft Press transform the raw material of my manuscript into finished form. Special thanks to Victoria Thulman, project editor, for her wonderful forbearance and resiliency in accommodating an author who has opinions about every facet of book production. Thanks to Kim Eggleston for the book's spare, elegant design, and to the rest of the Microsoft Press staff, including David Clark, Abby Hall, Cheryl Penner, and Michael Victor.

Thanks finally to my wife, Tammy, for her unmatchable moral support and trademark good humor. (This is number three, so now you have to think of a new joke. Fa!)

PRELIMINARY
SURVIVAL BRIEFING

About two million people are working on about 300,000 software projects in the United States at this time.[1] Between one third and two thirds of those projects will exceed their schedule and budget targets before they are delivered. Of the most expensive software projects, about half will eventually be canceled for being out of control. Many more are canceled in subtle ways—they are left to wither on the vine, or their sponsors simply declare victory and leave the battlefield without any new software to show for their trouble. Whether you're a senior manager, an executive, a software client, a user representative, or a project leader, this book explains how to prevent your project from suffering these consequences.

Software projects fail for one of two general reasons: the project team lacks the knowledge to conduct a software project successfully, or the project team lacks the resolve to conduct a project effectively. This book cannot do much about the lack of resolve, but it does contain much of the knowledge needed to conduct a software project successfully.

The factors that make a software project successful are not especially technical. Software projects are sometimes viewed as mysterious entities that survive or perish based on the developers' success in chanting magic technical incantations. When asked why they delivered a component two weeks late, developers say things like, "We had to implement a 32-bit thunking layer to interface with our OCX interface." Faced with explanations like that, it is no wonder that people without deep technical expertise feel powerless to influence a software project's success.

---

1. Source citations and notes about related topics can be found in the "Notes" section at the end of the book.

The message of the *Software Project Survival Guide* is that software projects survive not because of detailed technical considerations like "thunking layers" but for much more mundane reasons. Software projects succeed or fail based on how carefully they are planned and how deliberately they are executed. The vast majority of software projects can be run in a deterministic way that virtually assures success. If a project's stakeholders understand the major issues that determine project success, they can ensure that their project reaches a successful conclusion. The person who keeps a software project headed in the right direction can be a technical manager or an individual software developer—it can also be a top manager, a client, an investor, an end-user representative, or any other concerned party.

WHO SHOULD READ THIS BOOK

This book is for anyone who has a stake in a software project's outcome.

TOP MANAGERS, EXECUTIVES, CLIENTS, INVESTORS, AND END-USER REPRESENTATIVES

Nonsoftware people are commonly given responsibility for overseeing the development of a software product. These people have backgrounds in sales, accounting, finance, law, engineering, or some other field. They might not have any formal authority to direct the project, but they will still be held accountable for seeing that the project goes smoothly. At a minimum, they are expected to sound an alarm if the project begins to go awry.

If you're in this group, this book will provide you with a short, easily readable description of what a successful project looks like. It will give you many ways to tell in advance whether the project is headed for failure or success. It will also describe how to tell when no news is good news, when good news is bad news, or when good news really is good news.

PROJECT MANAGERS

Many software project managers are thrust into management positions without any training specific to managing software projects. If you're in this group, this book will help you master the key technical management skills of requirements management, software project planning, project tracking, quality assurance, and change control.

TECHNICAL LEADERS, PROFESSIONAL
DEVELOPERS, AND SELF-TAUGHT PROGRAMMERS

If you're an expert in technical details, you might not have had much exposure to the big-picture issues that project leaders need to focus on. In that case, you can think of this book as an annotated project plan. By providing an overview of a successful software project, this book will help you make the transition from expert technician to effective project leader. You can use the plan described in this book as a starting point, and you can tailor its strategies to the needs of your specific projects. If you've read *Rapid Development*, the first part of this book will be about half review for you. You might want to skim Chapters 1 through 5, read the end of Chapter 5 carefully, skim Chapter 6, and then begin reading carefully again starting with Chapter 7.

KINDS OF PROJECTS THIS BOOK COVERS

The plan will work for business systems, broad-distribution shrink-wrap software, vertical market systems, scientific systems, and similar programs. It is designed for use on desktop client/server projects using modern development practices such as object-oriented design and programming. It can easily be adapted for projects using traditional development practices and mainframe computers. The plan has been designed with project team sizes of 3 to 25 team members and schedules of 3 to 18 months in mind. These are considered to be medium-sized projects. If your project is smaller you can scale back some of this book's recommended practices. (Throughout the book, I point out places you can do that.)

This book is primarily intended for projects that are currently in the planning stages. If you're at the beginning of the project, you can use the approach as the basis for your project plan. If you're in the middle of a project, the Survival Test in Chapter 2 and the Survival Checks at the end of each chapter will help you determine your project's chance of success.

By itself, this book's plan is not formal or rigorous enough to support life-critical or safety-critical systems. It is appropriate for commercial applications and business software, and it is a marked improvement over many of the plans currently in use on multimillion-dollar projects.

A NOTE TO ADVANCED TECHNICAL READERS

The *Software Project Survival Guide* describes one effective way to conduct a software project. It is not the only effective way to run a project, and for any specific project it might not be the optimum way. The extremely knowledge-able technical leader will usually be able to come up with a better, fuller, more customized development plan than the generic one described here. But the plan described here will work much better than a hastily thrown together plan or no plan at all, and no plan at all is the most common alternative.

The plan described in the following chapters has been crafted to address the most common weaknesses that software projects face. It is loosely based on the "key process areas" identified by the Software Engineering Institute (SEI) in Level 2 of the SEI Capability Maturity Model. The SEI has identified these key processes as the critical factors that enable organizations to meet their schedule, budget, quality, and other targets. About 85 percent of all organizations perform below Level 2, and this plan will support dramatic improvements in those organizations. The SEI has defined the key process areas of Level 2 as follows:

◆ Project planning

◆ Requirements management

◆ Project tracking and oversight

◆ Configuration management

◆ Quality assurance

◆ Subcontract management

This book addresses all of these areas except subcontract management.

THIS BOOK'S FOUNDATION

In writing this book, I have kept three primary references at my elbow that have been invaluable resources, in addition to the many other resources I've drawn from. I've tried to condense the contents of these three references and present them in the most useful way that I can.

The first reference is the Software Engineering Institute's *Key Practices of the Capability Maturity Model, Version 1.1*. This book is a gold mine of hard-won industry experience in prioritizing implementation of new develop-ment practices. At almost 500 pages it is somewhat long, and even at that length the information is still dense. It is not a tutorial and so is not intended for the novice reader. But for someone who has a basic understanding of the practices it describes, the summary and structure that *Key Practices* provides is a godsend. This book is available free on the Internet at *http://www.sei.cmu.edu/* or from the National Technical Information Service (NTIS) branch of the U.S. Department of Commerce in Springfield, Virginia.

The second reference is the NASA Software Engineering Laboratory's (SEL's) *Recommended Approach to Software Development, Revision 3*. The SEL was the first organization to receive the IEEE Computer Society's Process Achievement Award. Many keys to the success of its process are described in the *Recommended Approach*. Whereas the SEI's document describes a set of practices without showing how to apply them to a specific project, the *Recommended Approach* describes a structured sequence of practices. The two volumes together form a complementary set. This book is also available free on the Internet at *http://fdd.gsfc.nasa.gov/seltext.html*.

The final "book" at my elbow has been my own experience. I am writing not as an academician who wants to create a perfect theoretical framework, but as a practitioner who wants to create a practical reference that will aid me in my work and my clients in theirs. The information drawn together here will make it easier for me to plan and conduct my next project and easier to explain its critical success factors to my clients. I hope it does the same for you.

Steve McConnell
Bellevue, Washington
August 1997

I

THE SURVIVAL MIND-SET

1
Welcome to Software Project Survival Training

Survival prospects for software projects are often poor, but they do not need to be. The first step in surviving a software project is being sure to begin the project in a civilized way. From that starting point, much more than mere survival is possible.

O ur standards for software *product* performance are unbelievably exacting compared to our standards for software *project* performance. The software user community expects software products to run for hours without crashing, executing millions of source code instructions with few or no errors. But the software development community expects far less from its projects. Users and clients might complain if a project is delivered one month, three months, or six months late, if it's hard to use, or if it lacks a few critical functions. But if the bulk of the planned software product is delivered at all—at any cost—*ever*—most software consumers will consider that project to be a success. We have suffered so many failed projects that the only outcome we really consider to be a failure is total collapse.

The upper echelons of the software industry have understood for many years what is needed to perform at a much higher level than is currently practiced. A successful project should be one that meets its cost, schedule, and quality goals within engineering tolerances and without padding its schedule or budget. After detailed plans have been made, the current state of the art supports meeting project goals within plus or minus 10 percent or better. This level of performance is currently within the reach of the average software project manager, and in many cases can be substantially influenced by project "outsiders"—upper managers, executives, clients, investors, and end-user representatives.

As chief software engineer at Construx Software Builders, I have been asked to review many failed projects. To the trained eye, the reasons for failure are usually apparent. Failure of medium-size software projects (those with 20,000–250,000 lines of source code) is almost always avoidable. Moreover, I have found that software projects can be optimized to meet any of several goals: shortest schedule, least cost, best quality, or any other goal. Not all of these goals can be achieved simultaneously, and the approach described in this book strikes a careful balance among these objectives so that a high-quality product can be delivered according to an efficient schedule at moderate cost.

SURVIVAL NEEDS

The first step in software project survival is recognizing a software project's essential survival needs. Abraham Maslow observed that human beings respond to a hierarchy of needs that involve a natural progression from lower motives to higher ones. The lowest level needs are called "survival needs," because they address physical needs that must be satisfied for a human being to exist at all. The lower motives, which are illustrated in Figure 1-1 as the motives below the dashed line, must be satisfied before we can progress to the higher motives. Thus physiological needs for food, air, and water must be satisfied before we can be motivated by the need for "belongingness" and love, self-esteem, or self-actualization.

I have found—along with many software experts—that a similar hierarchy of needs applies to software projects. Software projects have a set of basic survival needs that must be satisfied before it becomes possible for the project team to focus effectively on the project's higher level needs. And the higher levels of the pyramid are where dramatic improvements in quality and productivity take place.

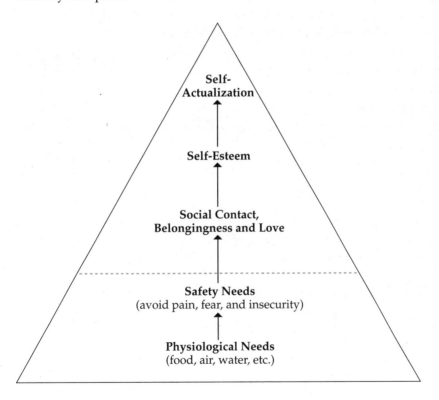

FIGURE 1-1   *Maslow's human need hierarchy. Lower level needs must be satisfied before higher level needs can be addressed.*

A project team must be satisfied that the project can be completed *at all*, for example, before it will begin to worry about whether it will be completed within plus or minus 10 percent of its schedule and budget targets. A project team must be capable of delivering software on time before it will become capable of optimizing a software project to meet an aggressive schedule with a limited budget—and advance the state of the art all at the same time.

As Figure 1-2 illustrates, the needs of the software project hierarchy are not exactly the same as the needs of individual project participants. A developer, for example, will typically prioritize his or her individual self-esteem above the need for healthy team dynamics. But the project typically has a greater need for healthy team dynamics than it has a need for the high self-esteem of individual team members.

This book focuses on the lower levels of the software project need hierarchy, reaching into the higher levels mainly when a higher-level need must be addressed before a lower-level need can be satisfied.

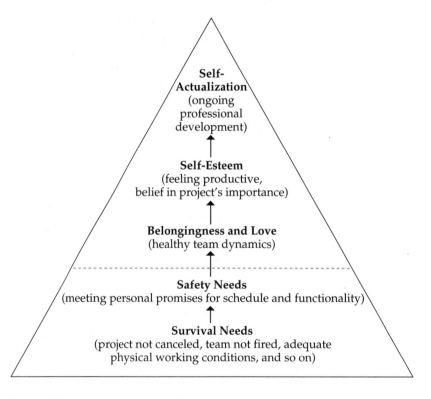

FIGURE 1-2   *Software project need hierarchy. Needs of the project are only approximately the same as the needs of the project's participants.*

SURVIVAL RIGHTS

A struggling project threatens each party's survival needs. The customer worries whether the project will be delivered too late to serve its intended purpose, delivered at prohibitive cost, or delivered at all. The manager worries whether the customer will cancel the project and make him look like a failure, or whether the developers are even capable of completing the project. The developer worries whether she will lose her job or be forced to sacrifice hundreds of hours of leisure time to show she is committed to the project. In each of these circumstances, the individuals retreat to the lower levels of the project need hierarchy—focusing on the safety need of meeting their personal promises. But this reaction causes the individuals to abandon the higher levels of the pyramid that must be exercised to achieve top quality and productivity.

As Thomas Hobbes observed in the 17th century, life under mob rule is solitary, poor, nasty, brutish, and short. Life on a poorly run software project is solitary, poor, nasty, brutish, and hardly ever short enough. The first step toward surviving a software project is for all parties to agree to treat one another in a civilized way. I've summarized some of the rules of civilization as they apply to software projects in the form of a "Customer's Bill of Rights." (In some cases, the project will not have a customer per se. In those cases, these rights may belong to the product manager, marketing representative, or end-user representative instead of the customer.)

CUSTOMER'S BILL OF RIGHTS

I have the right:

1. To set objectives for the project and have them followed

2. To know how long the software project will take and how much it will cost

3. To decide which features are in and which are out of the software

4. To make reasonable changes to requirements throughout the course of the project and to know the costs of making those changes

5. To know the project's status clearly and confidently

6. To be apprised regularly of risks that could affect cost, schedule, or quality, and to be provided with options for addressing potential problems

7. To have ready access to project deliverables throughout the project

The rights I'm most familiar with are the rights enumerated in the United States Bill of Rights. Those rights are not just "nice to have" but are essential to the operation of a representative democracy. Similarly, these software project rights do not just make a software project more enjoyable; they are required for it to work at all.

Another software project concept aligned with the United States Bill of Rights is the assumption that one person's software project *rights* are another person's software project *responsibilities*. We all enjoy the right to free speech, but the price we pay for that right is tolerating other people's right to free speech, even when we disagree with what they say or find it offensive. On a software project, customers must pay for their rights by respecting the project team's rights, which are listed here.

PROJECT TEAM'S BILL OF RIGHTS

I have the right:

1. To know the project objectives and to clarify priorities.

2. To know in detail what product I'm supposed to build and to clarify the product definition if it is unclear.

3. To have ready access to the customer, manager, marketer, or other person responsible for making decisions about the software's functionality.

4. To work each phase of the project in a technically responsible way, especially to not be forced to start coding too early in the project.

5. To approve effort and schedule estimates for any work that I will be asked to perform. This includes the right to provide only the kinds of cost and schedule estimates that are theoretically possible at each stage of the project; to take the time needed to create meaningful estimates; and to revise estimates whenever the project's requirements change.

6. To have my project's status reported accurately to customers and upper management.

7. To work in a productive environment free from frequent interruptions and distractions, especially during critical parts of the project.

The first step toward project success is getting all parties to respect the rights that make a successful project possible. The second step is to conduct the project in such a way that each party's survival needs are thoroughly satisfied and none of the parties feels threatened. How to do that is the subject of the rest of the book.

SURVIVAL CHECKS

Survival Checks appear at the end of each chapter. They refer to project characteristics that you can check from outside the project to gauge the health of the project.

Keys to success are marked with a thumbs-up symbol (). Projects that exhibit these characteristics are headed for success. Potential pitfalls are indented and marked with a bomb symbol (). Projects that exhibit these characteristics are at risk.

Survival Check

 The project team's survival needs are being met.

 The customer and the project team agree to respect each other's software project rights.

 The agreement in principle is not followed in practice.

2
Software Project Survival Test

A short test can assess a software project's health. If the test indicates the project is at risk, you can improve its condition by taking steps to raise its score.

This chapter contains a test you can use to assess a project's chances of successful completion. Will it be delivered on time and within budget? Will it be a glorious achievement or an embarrassing mistake? The work you do on this test can help you find out.

SURVIVAL TEST QUESTIONS

Give the project 3 points for each "yes" answer. Give the project partial credit if you feel that is most accurate—for example, give it 2 points for "probably" and 1 point for "kind of, but not really." If the project is in the early stages, answer the questions based on the project plans. If the project is well underway, answer the questions based on what has actually happened on the project. The section following the test explains how to interpret the score.[1]

SURVIVAL TEST

REQUIREMENTS

_____ 1.   Does the project have a clear, unambiguous vision statement or mission statement?

_____ 2.   Do all team members believe the vision is realistic?

_____ 3.   Does the project have a business case that details the business benefit and how the benefit will be measured?

_____ 4.   Does the project have a user interface prototype that realistically and vividly demonstrates the functionality that the actual system will have?

_____ 5.   Does the project have a detailed, written specification of what the software is supposed to do?

_____ 6.   Did the project team interview people who will actually use the software (end users) early in the project and continue to involve them throughout the project?

---

1. This test is available in electronic form on the _Survival Guide_ Web site. The site address is _http://www.construx.com/survivalguide/_.

PLANNING

____ 7. Does the project have a detailed, written Software Development Plan?

____ 8. Does the project's task list include creation of an installation program, conversion of data from previous versions of the system, integration with third-party software, meetings with the customer, and other "minor" tasks?

____ 9. Were the schedule and budget estimates officially updated at the end of the most recently completed phase?

____ 10. Does the project have detailed, written architecture and design documents?

____ 11. Does the project have a detailed, written Quality Assurance Plan that requires design and code reviews in addition to system testing?

____ 12. Does the project have a detailed Staged Delivery Plan for the software, which describes the stages in which the software will be implemented and delivered?

____ 13. Does the project's plan include time for holidays, vacation days, sick days, and ongoing training, and are resources allocated at less than 100 percent?

____ 14. Was the project plan, including the schedule, approved by the development team, the quality assurance team, and the technical writing team—in other words, the people responsible for doing the work?

PROJECT CONTROL

____ 15. Has a single key executive who has decision-making authority been made responsible for the project, and does the project have that person's active support?

____ 16. Does the project manager's workload allow him or her to devote an adequate amount of time to the project?

(continued)

____ 17.   Does the project have well-defined, detailed milestones ("binary milestones") that are considered to be either 100 percent done or 100 percent not done?

____ 18.   Can a project stakeholder easily find out which of these binary milestones have been completed?

____ 19.   Does the project have a feedback channel by which project members can anonymously report problems to their own managers and upper managers?

____ 20.   Does the project have a written plan for controlling changes to the software's specification?

____ 21.   Does the project have a Change Control Board that has final authority to accept or reject proposed changes?

____ 22.   Are planning materials and status information for the project—including effort and schedule estimates, task assignments, and progress compared to the plan thus far—available to every team member?

____ 23.   Is all source code placed under automated revision control?

____ 24.   Does the project environment include the basic tools needed to complete the project, including defect tracking software, source code control, and project management software?

RISK MANAGEMENT

____ 25.   Does the project plan articulate a list of current risks to the project? Has the list been updated recently?

____ 26.   Does the project have a project risk officer who is responsible for identifying emerging risks to the project?

____ 27.   If the project uses subcontractors, does it have a plan for managing each subcontract organization and a single person in charge of each one? (Give the project full score if it doesn't use subcontractors.)

PERSONNEL

_____ 28. Does the project team have all the technical expertise needed to complete the project?

_____ 29. Does the project team have expertise with the business environment in which the software will operate?

_____ 30. Does the project have a technical leader capable of leading the project successfully?

_____ 31. Are there enough people to do all the work required?

_____ 32. Does everyone work well together?

_____ 33. Is each person committed to the project?

TOTAL

_____ *Preliminary score.* Add up the points next to each answer.

_____ *Size multiplier.* Write in 1.5 if the project team has 3 or fewer full-time–equivalent people including developers, quality assurance personnel, and first-level management. Write in 1.25 if it has 4 to 6 full-time–equivalent people. Otherwise, write in 1.0.

_____ *Final score.* Multiply the preliminary score by the size multiplier.

INTERPRETING THE SURVIVAL TEST

This is a difficult test for most projects; many will score less than 50 points. Table 3-1 on the following page explains how to interpret the score.

The Software Project Survival Test establishes a measurement baseline you can use for future comparisons. It is similar to the kind of test you take at the beginning of a class in school. After you take the test, you spend a term studying and learning a new subject, and at the end of the term, you take the test again. If the instructor has done a good job of teaching the class (and you have done a good job of taking it), your score will improve.

TABLE 3-1   SCORING THE SURVIVAL TEST

Score	Comments
90+ Outstanding	A project with this score is virtually guaranteed to succeed in all respects, meeting its schedule, budget, quality, and other targets. In terms of Chapter 1's project needs hierarchy, such a project is fully "self-actualized."
80–89 Excellent	A project at this level is performing much better than average. Such a project has a high probability of delivering its software close to its schedule, budget, and quality targets.
60–79 Good	A score in this range represents a better-than-average level of software development effectiveness. Such a project stands a fighting chance of meeting either its schedule or its budget target, but it probably won't meet both.
40–59 Fair	This score is typical. A project with this score will likely experience high stress and shaky team dynamics, and the software will ultimately be delivered with less functionality than desired at greater cost and with a longer schedule. This kind of project stands to experience the greatest benefit from applying the plan described in this book.
< 40 At Risk	A project with this score has significant weaknesses in the major areas of requirements, planning, project control, risk management, and personnel. The primary concern of a project in this category should be whether it will finish at all.

To be a good "before and after" test, the test should cover the entire subject of the class. The Survival Test does cover the entire subject of software project survival. After reading this book, plan your next project and then take the survival test again. The project's score will have improved, and the project's chance of surviving will have improved with it.

Survival Check

 The project scores at least 60 on the Survival Test.

 The project scores less than 60, but corrective actions are planned to improve its score.

 The project team doesn't follow through on the planned corrective actions.

3 Survival Concepts

Well-defined development processes are important and necessary elements of software project survival. With well-defined processes, software personnel can spend most of their time on productive work that moves the project steadily toward completion. With poorly planned processes, developers spend a lot of their time correcting mistakes. Much of the leverage for project success is contained in upstream activities, and knowledgeable software stakeholders ensure that projects focus enough attention on upstream activities to minimize problems downstream.

B efore you begin a mission, you are briefed about its most important characteristics. This chapter describes the critical factors that contribute to software mission success.

The Power of "Process"

This book is about using effective software development processes. The phrase "software processes" can mean a lot of different things. Here are some examples of what I mean by "software processes:"

- Committing all requirements to writing.

- Using a systematic procedure to control additions and changes to the software's requirements.

- Conducting systematic technical reviews of all requirements, designs, and source code.

- Developing a systematic Quality Assurance Plan in the very early stages of the project that includes a test plan, review plan, and defect tracking plan.

- Creating an implementation plan that defines the order in which the software's functional components will be developed and integrated.

- Using automated source code control.

- Revising cost and schedule estimates as each major milestone is achieved. Milestones include the completion of requirements analysis, architecture, and detailed design as well as the completion of each implementation stage.

These processes are beneficial in ways that will shortly become apparent.

Negative View of Process

The word "process" is viewed as a four-letter word by some people in the software development community. These people see "software processes" as rigid, restrictive, and inefficient. They think that the best way to run a project is to hire the best people you can, give them all the resources they ask for, and turn them loose to let them do what they're best at. According to this view, projects that run without any attention to process can run extremely efficiently. People who hold this view imagine that the relationship between work and productivity over the course of a project looks like the chart shown in Figure 3-1 on the facing page.

People who hold this view acknowledge that some amount of "thrashing," or unproductive work, will take place. Developers will make mistakes, they agree, but they will be able to correct them quickly and efficiently—certainly at less overall cost than the cost of "process."

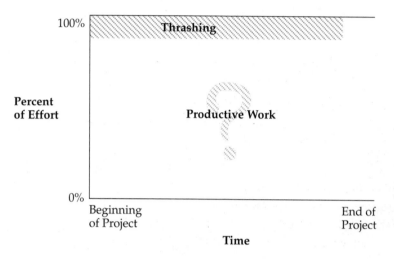

FIGURE 3-1 *Mistaken perception that ignoring process increases the proportion of productive work on projects.*

Adding process, then, is thought to be pure overhead and simply takes time away from productive work, as shown in Figure 3-2.

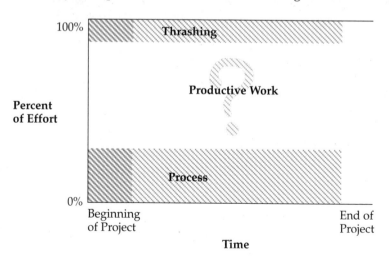

FIGURE 3-2 *Mistaken perception that an attention to process will decrease the proportion of productive work. (Process is seen as pure overhead.)*

This point of view has intuitive appeal. At the beginning of a project (shown by the darker shaded areas), a focus on process certainly does take time away from productive work. If that trend continued throughout a project (shown by the lighter shaded areas), it wouldn't make sense to spend much time on process.

Software industry experience with medium-size projects, however, has revealed that the trend shown in Figure 3-2 does not continue throughout the project. Projects that don't pay attention to establishing effective processes early on are forced to slap them together later, when slapping them together takes more time and does less good. Here are some scenarios that illustrate why earlier is better:

- *Change control.* In the middle of the project, team members informally agree to implement a wide variety of changes that are directly proposed to them by their manager or customer. They don't begin controlling changes systematically until late in the project. By that time, the scope of the product has expanded by 25 to 50 percent or more, and the budget and the schedule have expanded accordingly.

- *Quality assurance.* Projects that don't set up processes to eliminate defects in early stages fall into extended test-debug-reimplement-retest cycles that seem interminable. So many defects are reported by testing that by the end of the project, the "change control board" or "feature team" may be meeting as often as every day to prioritize defect corrections. Because of the vast number of defects, the software has to be released with many known (albeit low priority) defects. In the worst case, the software might never reach a level of quality high enough for it to be released.

- *Uncontrolled revisions.* Major defects discovered late in the project can cause the software to be redesigned and rewritten during testing. Since no one planned to rewrite the software during testing, the project deviates so far from its plans that it essentially runs without any planning or control.

◆   *Defect tracking.* Defect tracking isn't set up until late in the project. Some reported defects are not fixed simply because they are forgotten, and the software is released with these defects even though they would have been easy to fix.

◆   *System integration.* Components developed by different developers are not integrated with one another until the end of the project. By the time the components are integrated, the interfaces between components are out of synch and much work must be done to bring them back into alignment.

◆   *Automated source code control.* Source code revision control isn't established until late in the project, after developers have begun to lose work by accidentally overwriting the master copies of their own or one another's source code files.

◆   *Scheduling.* On projects that are behind schedule, developers are asked to reestimate their remaining work as often as once a week or more, taking time away from their development work.

When a project has paid too little early attention to the processes it will use, by the end of a project developers feel that they are spending all of their time sitting in meetings and correcting defects and little or no time extending the software. They know the project is thrashing. When developers see they are not meeting their deadlines, their survival impulses kick in and they retreat to "solo development mode," focusing exclusively on their personal deadlines. They withdraw from interactions with managers, customers, testers, technical writers, and the rest of the development team, and project coordination unravels.

Far from a steady level of productive work suggested by Figure 3-1, the medium-size project conducted without much attention to development processes typically experiences the pattern shown in Figure 3-3 on the next page.

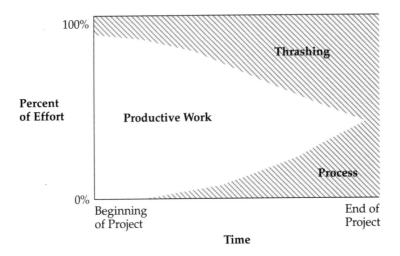

FIGURE 3-3   *Real experience of projects that pay little attention to process. As the project environment becomes increasingly complicated, thrashing and process both increase.*

In this pattern, projects experience a steady increase in thrashing over the course of a project. By the middle of the project, the team realizes that it is spending a lot of time thrashing and that some attention to process would be beneficial. But by then much of the damage has been done. The project team tries to increase the effectiveness of its process, but its efforts hold the level of thrashing steady, at best. In some cases, the late attempt to improve the project's processes actually makes the thrashing worse.

The lucky projects release their software while they are still eking out a small amount of productive work. The unlucky projects can't complete their software before reaching a point at which 100 percent of their time is spent on process and thrashing. After spending several weeks or months in this condition, such a project is typically canceled when management or the customer realizes that the project is no longer moving forward. If you think that attention to process is needless overhead, consider that the overhead of a canceled project is 100·percent.

PROCESS TO THE RESCUE

Fortunately, there are a variety of alternatives to this dismal scenario, and the best do not rely at all on rigid, inefficient processes (also known as R.I.P.). Some processes certainly are rigid and inefficient, but I don't recommend that projects use them. The approach described in this book requires use of processes that *increase* the project's flexibility and efficiency.

When these kinds of processes are used, the project profile looks like the one shown in Figure 3-4.

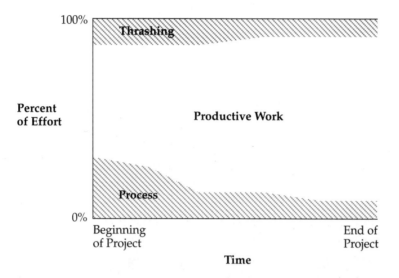

FIGURE 3-4   *Experience of projects that focus early attention on process. As the team gains experience with its processes and fine tunes them to the working environment, the time spent on process and thrashing both diminish.*

During the first few weeks of the project, the process-oriented team will seem less productive than the process-phobic team because the level of thrashing will be the same on both projects, and the process-oriented team will be spending a significant amount of its time on processes.

By the middle of the project, the team that focused on process early will have reduced the level of thrashing compared to the beginning of the project, and will have streamlined its processes. At that point, the process-phobic team will be just beginning to realize that thrashing is a significant problem and just beginning to institute some processes of its own.

By the end of the project, the process-oriented team will be operating at a high-speed hum, with little thrashing, and it will be performing its processes with little conscious effort. This team tolerates a small amount of thrashing because eliminating the last bit of thrashing would cost more in overhead than would be saved. When all is said and done, the overall effort on the project will be considerably lower than the effort of the process-phobic team.

———◆———

*An investment made in process at the beginning
of the project produces large returns
later in the project.*

———◆———

Organizations that have explicitly focused on improving their development processes have, over several years, cut their time-to-market by about one-half and reduced their costs and defects by factors of 3 to 10. Over a 5-year period, Lockheed cut its development costs by 75 percent, reduced its time-to-market by 40 percent, and reduced its defects by 90 percent. Over a 6.5-year period, Raytheon tripled its productivity and realized a return on investment (ROI) in process improvement of almost 8 to 1. Bull HN realized an ROI of 4 to 1 after 4 years of software process improvement efforts, and Schlumberger realized an ROI of almost 9 to 1 after 3.5 years of software process improvement. NASA's Software Engineering Laboratory cut its average cost per mission by 50 percent and its defect rate by 75 percent over an 8-year period while dramatically increasing the complexity of software used on each mission. Similar results have been reported at Hughes, Loral, Motorola, Xerox and other companies that have focused on systematically improving their software processes.

Here's the best news: Can you guess the average cost of these improvements in productivity, quality, and schedule performance? It's about 2 percent of total development costs—typically about $1,500 per developer per year.

PROCESS VS. CREATIVITY AND MORALE

One of the common objections to putting systematic processes in place is that they will limit programmers' creativity. Programmers do indeed have a high need to be creative. Managers and project sponsors also have a need for projects to be predictable, to provide progress visibility, and to meet schedule, budget, and other targets.

The criticism that systematic processes limit developers' creativity is based on the mistaken idea that there is some inherent contradiction between developers' creativity and the satisfaction of management objectives. It is certainly possible to create an oppressive environment in which programmer creativity and management goals are placed at odds, and many companies have done that, but it is just as possible to set up an environment in which those goals are in harmony and can be achieved simultaneously.

Companies that have focused on process have found that effective processes support creativity and morale. In a survey of about 50 companies, only 20 percent of the people in the least process-oriented companies rated their staff morale as "good" or "excellent." In organizations that paid more attention to their software processes, about 50 percent of the people rated their staff morale as good or excellent. And in the most process-sophisticated organizations, 60 percent of the people rated their morale as good or excellent.

Programmers feel best when they're most productive. Good project leadership establishes a clear vision and then puts a process framework into place that allows programmers to feel incredibly productive. Programmers dislike weak leadership that provides too little structure because they end up working at cross purposes and, inevitably, are forced to throw away huge chunks of their work. Programmers appreciate enlightened leadership that emphasizes predictability, visibility, and control.

The appropriate response to the so-called contradiction between process and creativity is that none of the processes described in this book will limit programmers' creativity in any way that matters. Most provide a supporting structure that will free programmers to be more creative about the technical work that matters and free them from the distractions that typically consume their attention on poorly run projects.

Transitioning to a Systematic Process

If a project team isn't currently using a systematic process, one of the easiest ways to transition to one is to map out the current software development process, identify the parts of that process that aren't working, and then try to fix those parts. Although project teams will sometimes claim that they don't currently have a process, every project team has a process of some kind. (If they claim not to have one, they probably just don't have a very good one.)

The least sophisticated process typically looks like this:

1.   Discuss the software that needs to be written.

2.   Write some code.

3.   Test the code to identify the defects.

4.   Debug to find root causes of defects.

5.   Fix the defects.

6.   If the project isn't done yet, return to step 1.

This book describes a more sophisticated and more effective software process.

One obstacle to creating a systematic software process is that project teams are afraid they will err on the side of having too much process—that their process will be overly bureaucratic and create too much overhead for the project. This is typically not a significant risk for several reasons:

◆   A project that uses the approach described in this book will have a fairly sophisticated process without incurring much overhead.

◆   Software projects are often larger than they at first appear. Far more projects err on the side of too little process than too much.

◆   Starting with too much process and loosening some of the processes later on, if needed, is easier than starting with too little process and trying to add additional processes once a project is under way.

◆   The cost and schedule penalty for having too much process is far smaller than the penalty for having too little process, for reasons I will explain next.

UPSTREAM, DOWNSTREAM

Good software processes are designed to root out problems early in the project. This concept is important enough to discuss in some detail.

You'll sometimes hear experienced software developers talk about the "upstream" and "downstream" parts of a software project. The word "upstream" simply refers to the early parts of a project such as requirements development and architecture, and "downstream" refers to the later parts such as construction and system testing.

I have found that this distinction between "upstream" and "down-stream" is a fundamentally useful way to think about a software project. The work developers do early in the project is placed into a stream and has to be fished back out later in the project. If the early work is done well, the work that's fished out later is healthy and contributes to project success. If the early work is done poorly, the work that's fished out later can severely impair the project. In extreme circumstances, it can prevent the project from ever getting finished.

Researchers have found that an error inserted into the project stream early—for example, an error in requirements specification or architecture—tends to cost 50 to 200 times as much to correct late in the project as it does to correct close to the point where it was originally put into the stream. Figure 3-5 illustrates this effect.

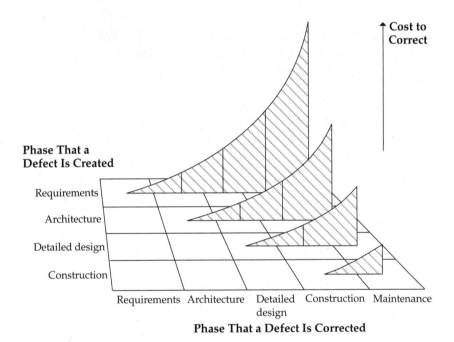

FIGURE 3-5   *Increase in defect cost as time between defect creation and defect correction increases. Effective projects practice "phase containment"—the detection and correction of defects in the same phase in which they are created.*

One sentence in a requirements specification can easily turn into several design diagrams. Later in the project, those diagrams can turn into hundreds of lines of source code, dozens of test cases, many pages of end-user documentation, help screens, instructions for technical support personnel, and so on.

If the project team has an opportunity to correct a mistake at requirements time when the only work that has been done is the creation of a one-sentence requirements statement, it makes good sense for the team to correct that statement rather than to correct all the various manifestations of the inadequate requirements statement downstream. This idea is sometimes called "phase containment," and refers to the detection and correction of defects in the same phase in which the defects are introduced.

———◆———

Successful project teams create their own
opportunities to correct upstream problems
by conducting thorough, careful reviews of
requirements and architecture.

———◆———

Because no code is generated while the upstream activities are conducted, these activities might seem as though they are delaying "the real work" of the project. In reality, they are doing just the opposite. They are laying the groundwork for the project's success.

Erring on the side of too much process will marginally increase the project's overhead, but erring on the side of too little allows defects to slip through that must be corrected at 50 to 200 times the efficient cost of correcting them. For this reason, the smart money errs on the side of too much process rather than on the side of too little.

CONE OF UNCERTAINTY

One of the reasons that mistakes made early in a project cost 50 to 200 times as much to correct downstream as upstream is that the upstream decisions tend to be farther reaching than the downstream decisions.

Early in the project, a project team addresses the large issues like whether to support Windows NT and the Macintosh or just Windows NT, and whether to provide fully customizable reports or fixed format reports. In the middle of the project, a project team addresses medium-size issues, such as how many subsystems to have, how in general to handle error-processing, and how to adapt a printing routine from an old project to the current project. Late in the project, a project team addresses small issues, such as which technical algorithm to use and whether to allow the user to cancel an operation when it's partway complete. As the cone of uncertainty in Figure 3-6 suggests, software development is a process of continuous refinement, which proceeds from large grain to small grain, from large decisions to small decisions. The time burned on a software project is the time required to think through and make these decisions. Decisions made at one stage of the project affect the next set of decisions.

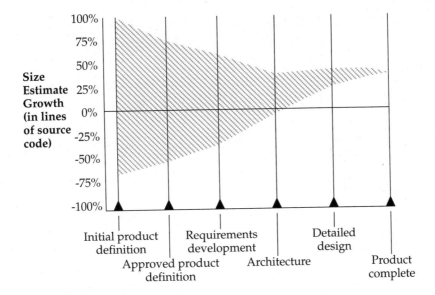

FIGURE 3-6   *Cone of uncertainty. Decision-making on a software project progresses from large grain to small grain. The project team can't know much about the decisions to be made in a specific phase until it has completed most of the work for the phase that immediately precedes it.*

Before the project team has actually made the first set of decisions, it can only make the most general educated guess about the decisions that will be made later in the project. After the set of decisions at one level of granularity have been made, a team can make pretty accurate estimates of the kinds of decisions that will need to be made at the next level of granularity. The project team makes the best decisions it can at the large-grain level, but sometimes unforeseen (and unforeseeable) issues at the fine-grain level percolate back up to a larger context, and the need to cancel an operation when it's partway complete means that the project team has to redesign a routine, a module, or a subsystem.

If you want to understand what software development is all about, you need to understand that the project team has to think through and make all the decisions in one stage before it can know enough about the next stage even to estimate the work involved in it.

IMPLICATIONS FOR PROJECT ESTIMATION

The cone of uncertainty has strong implications for software project estimation. It implies that it is not only difficult to estimate a project accurately in the early stages, it is *theoretically impossible*. At the end of the requirements development phase, the scope of the project will be determined by myriad decisions yet to be made during architecture, detailed design, and construction. The person who claims to be able to *estimate* the impact of those myriad decisions before they are actually made is either a prophet or not very well informed about the intrinsic nature of software development.

On the other hand, the person who seeks to *control* the way those decisions are made in order to meet the project's schedule or budget targets is operating sensibly. You can set firm schedule and budget targets early in the project as long as you're willing to be ruthless about cutting planned functionality to meet those targets. Keys to success in meeting targets in this way include setting crystal clear and non-conflicting goals at the beginning of the project, keeping the product concept very flexible, and then actively tracking and controlling development work throughout the rest of the project.

———◆———

*Early in the project you can have
firm cost and schedule targets
or a firm feature set, but not both.*

———◆———

Survival Check

👍 Project leadership understands the critical role of well-defined processes and supports them.

👍 The project's processes are generally oriented toward detecting as many problems upstream as possible.

👍 Project leadership recognizes that estimates made during the first half of the project are inherently imprecise and will need to be refined as the project progresses.

4 Survival Skills

Software projects are inherently complex, and complex projects cannot succeed without careful planning. A well-planned project will be actively controlled, its progress will be visible, and its people will be given the support they need to do the project's work. Software projects are also inherently risky, and they cannot succeed without active risk management. Involving users in the project early and continuously, striving to hold the product to the minimal sufficient feature set, and maintaining a focus on the desired result help to address key project risks.

S mall projects can succeed through sheer force of will and a bit of luck. Medium and large projects require a more systematic approach. This chapter outlines some of the skills needed to ensure that a medium-size project succeeds.

PLANNING

Many technical workers would rather do technical work than spend time planning. Many technical managers do not have sufficient training in technical management to feel confident that their planning will improve the project's outcome. Since neither party really wants to do the planning, it often doesn't get done.

But failure to plan is one of the most critical mistakes a project can make. Because of the upstream/downstream effect described in the last chapter, effective planning is needed to resolve problems upstream, at low cost, rather than downstream, at high cost. The average project spends about *80 percent* of its time on unplanned rework—fixing mistakes that were made earlier in the project.

Success in software development depends on making a carefully planned series of small mistakes in order to avoid making unplanned large mistakes. Exploring four design alternatives and discarding three of them amounts to making three small mistakes. Not doing enough design work and rewriting the code three times amounts to making three large mistakes. Because fixing upstream defects downstream costs 50 to 200 times as much as fixing them upstream, carefully orchestrated projects jump at the chance to fix as many mistakes as possible at the bargain price of 1/50 to 1/200 their potential cost.

Where do projects find the time to plan? It's easy. Take a small percentage of the time that most projects spend on unplanned rework and invest that early in the project to avoid doing extensive rework later. Not all the time spent on upstream activities will actually result in downstream savings, but much of it will. A good rule of thumb for upstream quality assurance activities is that each hour spent on activities such as technical reviews will save 3 to 10 hours of downstream costs. You could also look at this rule from a slightly different perspective: each day a developer spends reviewing project requirements or architecture will typically save the project 3 to 10 days later in the project.

EXAMPLES OF SOFTWARE PLANNING

How does a project team plan a project so that it can deliver software on a budget? Here are some of the specific features of a well-planned project:

- *A Software Development Plan.* This plan maps a course for the project. Committing the plan to writing allows the project's stakeholders to refer to the plan throughout the project.

- *Project estimates.* Project estimates provide a foundation for project plans. A careful estimate leads to scoping the project appropriately, which in turn leads to budgeting, staffing, and scheduling the project appropriately. A shoddy estimate can undercut the project in all these respects, making it difficult to complete the project successfully and impossible to complete it efficiently.

- *Revised estimates.* Revised estimates created at the end of each major phase of the project allow for mid-course corrections and help to keep the project on solid footing.

- *A Quality Assurance Plan.* A Quality Assurance Plan that includes both technical reviews and testing assures that the project will not succumb to a costly and defect-ridden test, debug, and correction cycle.

- *A Staged Delivery Plan.* A Staged Delivery Plan defines the order in which the software will be constructed. It ensures that the software solution is developed to both maximize the value to the customer at each stage and minimize the risks to the project.

In addition to the explicit planning activities I just listed, several of a software project's other major activities are also planning activities, though they aren't usually thought of that way.

- *Requirements development.* Requirements development identifies in detail the problem that the project team is trying to solve. It amounts to planning to solve the right problem.

- *Architecture.* Architecture is a high-level specification for the way in which the problem will be solved. It is a plan to build the right solution to the problem.

- *Detailed design.* Detailed design is a comprehensive plan of what the project is going to build. It is a plan to build the right solution in the right way.

Planning Checkpoint Review

Planning is so critical to the success of a project that some experts report that a project's ultimate success or failure is determined as early as 10 percent of the way through the project. Whether the exact number is 10 percent or some other number, very early in the project the project team should have produced a user interface prototype, detailed requirements, and a detailed project plan including careful cost and schedule estimates. That information can be used to make a "go/no go" decision about the project.

Two-Phase Funding Approach

One problem with software project funding in some organizations is that project managers have to ask for funding for the entire project before they have had a chance to complete much exploratory work. Such funding requests inevitably miss the mark because too little is known about the desired software to support creation of meaningful cost and schedule estimates. The software industry's experience is that estimates created at this early stage of a project are often off by as much as a factor of 4 on either the high or low side.

A better approach is for the project manager to request funding in two major phases. The project manager first requests funding for the exploratory phase during which the first 10 to 20 percent of the project is completed. At the end of that phase, the project team holds a Planning Checkpoint Review. In conjunction with that review, senior management or the customer makes a go/no go decision, and then the project manager requests funding for the remainder of the project. At this point the project cost could still vary greatly from the estimate, but the exploratory work that has been done will bring that variation down from a factor of 4 either way to more like plus or minus 50 percent.

Preparing for the Planning Checkpoint Review

Before the Planning Checkpoint Review can be held, the following materials, which are discussed in this book, need to be available:

- Name of project's key decision maker
- Vision statement
- Business case for the software
- Preliminary effort and schedule goals

- Preliminary effort and schedule estimates
- Top 10 Risks List
- User Interface Style Guide
- Detailed User Interface Prototype
- User Manual/Requirements Specification
- Software Quality Assurance Plan
- Detailed Software Development Plan

If these materials are not available, holding the Planning Checkpoint Review is pointless because there won't be enough information at hand to determine the project's viability. If the project team continues to be unable to create these materials, which support the Planning Checkpoint Review, it is safe to assume that the project is not being run effectively and faces a great risk of failure.

The exact amount of time required to create these materials will vary depending on how much work is needed to identify the software's requirements. In circumstances in which end users know exactly what software they want built, this period might take only 10 percent of the software's total development schedule. In more typical cases, creating these materials might take 10 to 20 percent of the total development schedule. On some projects, the hardest part of the job is helping the end users figure out what they want built, and so occasionally this part of the project can take 25 percent of the total development schedule or more. The initial funding request and plans for the Planning Checkpoint Review should take this variability in requirements work into account.

AGENDA FOR THE PLANNING CHECKPOINT REVIEW

The Planning Checkpoint Review should focus on the following topics:

- Is the original product concept still viable?
- Will it be possible to develop a product that matches the project's vision statement?
- Is the business case for the software still justified when the updated, more accurate cost and schedule estimates are considered?
- Can the major risks to the project be surmounted?

- Have users and developers been able to agree on a detailed User Interface Prototype?

- Is the User Manual/Requirements Specification complete and stable enough to support further development work?

- Is the Software Development Plan complete and adequate to support further development work?

- What is the estimated cost of completing the project?

- What is the estimated schedule for completing the project?

The work completed during the first 10 to 20 percent of the project should be sufficient to answer these questions, and the answers to these questions should give the client or top management enough information to decide whether to fund the second phase of the project.

Major Benefits of the Planning Checkpoint Review

Breaking software project funding into two major phases helps software organizations in at least three ways. First, it gives the organization an opportunity to look at canceling a project as a positive decision. We tend to view any canceled project as a failure, but a project canceled when it is only 10 to 20 percent complete should be considered a resounding success. Canceling one project that ultimately goes nowhere after it is 10 to 20 percent complete instead of 80 to 90 percent complete can pay for the exploratory phases of a lot of other projects.

Second, deferring the bulk of the funding request until after the project is 10 to 20 percent complete provides for much more reliable funding requests for the bulk of the project.

Third, requiring a project manager to complete 10 to 20 percent of a project before requesting funding for the rest of it forces the manager to focus on the upstream activities that are critical to the project's success. These activities are often abbreviated or ignored, and the damaging consequences of such neglect don't otherwise become apparent until late in the project when many defects have to be corrected at great cost downstream. If the project team is required to complete the most important upstream work before proceeding with downstream work, overall project risk can be substantially reduced.

RISK MANAGEMENT

A special kind of planning is risk management. Anyone who has been through a medium or large software project knows first-hand that dozens of things can go wrong. The most successful projects take active steps to avoid succumbing to such problems. You might be an optimist, but with software projects, as the saying goes, you can hope for the best but you should prepare for the worst.

Several of the most serious software project risks are directly related to planning:

◆   Failure to plan

◆   Failure to follow the plan that has been created

◆   Failure to revise the plan when project circumstances change

Not practicing active risk management on a software project is tantamount to ignoring decades of experience in which the software industry has learned thousands of times that software development is a high-risk activity. Many risks can be prevented or minimized by performing active risk management. Many of those same risks can cripple a project if not actively addressed.

The practices contained in this book's survival strategy (and discussed throughout the rest of the book) have been chosen because they involve less risk than alternative practices, or because they promote detection and control of other kinds of project risks. You don't really have a choice about whether to practice risk management on a software project. As Tom Gilb says, if you don't actively attack the risks on a software project, they will actively attack you.

PROJECT CONTROL

One theme of this book is that software projects can be controlled to meet their schedule, budget, and other targets. To some people, the idea of "controlling" a project sounds almost inhumane. They think it refers to controlling the people on the project, and it conjures up images of an oppressive project manager wielding authority with a whip and brass knuckles.

————◆————

*The opposite of "controlling" a project is having a
project that is literally out of control.*

————◆————

For some reason people think that it is somehow possible to have a
project that is under control without anyone or any group of people actually
controlling it. Both my brain and my experience tell me that is impossible.

Controlling a project refers to controlling the project itself, not to controlling the people. Here are some examples of what I mean by "control":

◆   Choosing a software life cycle model, such as the staged delivery
    model used in this book, to provide a framework for the project's
    technical work.

◆   Managing changes to requirements so that only necessary
    changes are accepted.

◆   Setting design and coding standards so that the designs and
    source code produced are consistent with each other.

◆   Creating a detailed plan for the project so each developer's work
    contributes to the goals of the project and doesn't conflict with
    other developers' work.

Control is not something that happens as a by-product of good technical work. Control needs to be built into the project explicitly through active project management and continuous, ongoing control activities. Specific
activities are discussed throughout the rest of the book.

PROJECT VISIBILITY

Closely related to project control is the concept of "visibility," which refers
to the ability to determine a project's true status. Is the project performing
within 10 percent of its schedule and budget targets, or within only 100
percent? Is the project on track to achieve its quality goals, or is it lagging
behind? If the project team can't answer such questions, it doesn't have
enough visibility to control its project.

Here are examples of activities that contribute to visibility:

- Using a vision statement or goals to set broad objectives for the project. If you don't know where you want the project to go, it probably won't go there.

- Holding a Planning Checkpoint Review after the project is 10 percent complete to determine whether the project is viable and should be completed.

- Regularly comparing actual performance against planned performance to determine whether the plan is working, corrective action needs to be taken, or the plan needs to be modified.

- Using binary milestones to determine whether tasks are done or not done. Milestones are considered either "100 percent done" or "100 percent not done," because allowing that little step from "100 percent done" to "90 percent done" has historically been found to reduce the quality of the status information from "very good" to "awful."

- Driving the product to a releasable state periodically to help determine the product's true condition and control its quality level.

- Revising estimates at the end of each project phase to support improved plans based on more information and better understood planning assumptions.

Many project teams have found the hard way that good visibility is not something they get automatically. If you want good visibility, the project team has to plan it into the project from the start, and if you want a successful project, you have to have good visibility.

PEOPLEWARE

Software development requires creativity, intelligence, initiative, persistence, and a great degree of internal motivation. Any effective approach to software development must remember that if the development team isn't on board, the project cannot possibly succeed. It might ship, but it will ship with low quality. Or it will ship without the spark of inspiration that differentiates a merely passable product from a great one. Or a substantial part of the development team will quit within a few weeks of releasing the product.

Tom DeMarco and Timothy Lister popularized the term "peopleware" to refer to software management practices that recognize the importance of the human role in software development. If you are not a software developer, some of the most important peopleware guidelines might surprise you.

Align Developers' Interests with Work Assignments

As a general rule, the single greatest motivator for an individual software developer is the alignment of interests with assigned work. Developers who find their work interesting are highly motivated, and those who find their work boring are demotivated. After 15 years of research, Robert Zawacki reported that about 60 percent of a developer's productivity comes from the match up between the job and the person. For best productivity, developers must be assigned to jobs they find stimulating.

——————◆——————

Some people are motivated by impossible goals.
Because developers pride themselves on being
realistic, they tend to be demotivated by goals
that are far out of reach.

——————◆——————

Show Developers That You Sincerely Appreciate Them

Like everyone else, developers like to be appreciated. If the project sponsors show they sincerely appreciate the developers, the developers' commitment to the project will tick up a notch. If developers think the display of appreciation is phony or manipulative, their commitment will tick down. Don't try to motivate developers with cheerleading campaigns, impossible challenges, or monetary rewards.

Provide Thinking-Oriented Office Space

Software development is a process of continuous discovery and invention. The atmosphere most supportive of that process is one that is relaxed and contemplative. Effective software development requires that developers achieve a level of concentration similar to that of a mathematician or physicist. Can you imagine Albert Einstein sitting at his desk while his manager berates him, "Albert, we need that theory of relatively *now*! Hurry up!" Since software developers aren't as smart as Albert Einstein, they need an even more supportive work environment.

Avoid Open Work Bays

A claim that surfaces from time to time is that open work bays encourage communication on software projects. The problem is that open work bays encourage incidental, unstructured communication that hurts productivity. Beneficial, incidental communication can be encouraged more effectively by installing a soda machine in a place where developers can bump into each other when they're not trying to concentrate on problems that demand their complete concentration. The claim in favor of the communication benefit arising from open work bays has an intuitive appeal but doesn't bear close examination, and the software research data indicates clearly that developers are most productive in one- or two-person offices.

For example, studies have found that productivity levels of developers who work in private, quiet, one- or two-person offices can be as much as 2.5 times as great as the productivity levels of developers who work in open work bays or cubicles. Software development is a deeply intellectual activity. It's hard to be intellectually effective with phones ringing, announcements blaring over the public address system, and people walking up to your cubicle every few minutes to ask questions on various topics.

———◆———

The job of the average manager requires a shift in focus every few minutes. The job of the average software developer requires that the developer not shift focus more often than every few hours.

———◆———

Many organizations are restricted in their ability to provide developers with quiet, private offices. Either their general office spaces simply do not have enough private offices for each developer to have one, or private offices are treated as VP-level status symbols, which makes it impossible to provide them to developers. Some organizations have found it effective to locate their software development teams in separate facilities where they can provide developers with the productive environments they need. Others improve their environments incrementally by letting developers work occasionally in private conference rooms, wear head phones to cut down on distractions, or work at home. Organizations that cannot find a way to provide developers with a quiet, private environment free from interruptions will have no choice but to adjust their productivity expectations sharply downward.

USER INVOLVEMENT

User involvement is critical to a software project in several respects. First, building software successfully hinges on building a product that end users will use and like. Software developers are notorious for crafting technically elegant solutions to problems that users don't care about. Marketers are notorious for overloading a software product with so many features that users can't find the few features they really need.

Second, there really is little magic involved in developing software products that users love. The project team simply needs to *ask the users what they want, show them what they intend to build, and ask them how they like it*— then listen carefully until they fully understand both the stated and unstated elements of the users' responses.

The project team may have to work at fully understanding what the user is asking for. Likewise, users might have to work at understanding how the project will come together—users must understand that the mock-ups developers show them to solicit their input are nowhere close to being the real software. Even identifying who "the user" is can be difficult. All these issues are discussed more in Chapter 8.

User involvement saves time because it eliminates one large source of requirements changes—the feature creep that arises from not defining the right software in the first place. If users aren't involved early on, when they are brought in to review the software late in the project, they identify ways in which the software has fallen short of their needs. At that point the development team is faced with a difficult choice: ignore the user input and adhere to the budget and schedule, or act on the user input in the downstream part of the project and throw the budget and schedule out the window. Typically a compromise is reached in which the easy changes are adopted and the hard changes are deferred to a later version. Clearly, it is better to involve users early on, while the software is malleable, and before a lot of work has been sunk into software the users don't want.

Because of this dynamic of late-discovery-of-user-needs followed by compromise-between-user-desires-and-schedule-and-budget, projects that involve users early on tend to deliver products that are thought by users to have higher quality than projects that do not involve users early on. Externally, the software better fits user needs and expectations, which is one kind of quality. Internally, the software contains fewer defects because there have been fewer changes in direction, and the product architecture, design, and implementation have been more stable. If the perceived user needs change throughout the project, internal software quality will degrade rapidly as developers are forced to cobble unforeseen functionality onto an existing framework that is ill-suited to support it.

In addition to early involvement, users need to be involved on an ongoing basis. Only rarely do software projects hit upon a really good solution on the first attempt. Typically, a software project must generate several versions of a user interface prototype before the users sit up and say, "Yes, that is the software I want." A good, mature user interface prototype can move a project most of the way toward delivering what end users want, but usability aspects of the software are inevitably refined as the software itself is developed. Building user-oriented checkpoints into the project helps the team make a set of small, inexpensive, mid-course corrections rather than one large, expensive correction at the end of the project. (This book's use of staged deliveries provides for such a series of mid-course corrections.)

User involvement doesn't have to break the bank. In *Usability Engineering*, Jakob Nielsen points out that the benefit-to-cost ratio is highest when about 3 usability testers are used. (The benefit-to-cost ratio remains positive up to about 15 testers.)

In 1994, the Standish Group conducted a review of more than 8000 software projects. Their review concluded that end-user involvement was the most significant project success factor. Among failed projects, lack of user input was the most significant failure factor. Experts in rapid development of computer software have stated that ready access to end users is one of the most critical success factors in rapid development projects.

———◆———

Involving users throughout the project is a critical
software project survival skill.

———◆———

Product Minimalism

In terms of the complexity of software components and their functionality, successful development of a software project requires a "less is more" orientation from requirements time through release. Because software development work is so mentally taxing, it becomes critical that people working on the project take active steps to make the project *as simple as possible* rather than needlessly complicated. Feature specifications, designs, and implementation should all emphasize simplicity. Many developers are attracted to complexity, so their tendency is sometimes to make the problem more complicated rather than less complicated. But success depends on finding ways to simplify the project.

Developers who look for the most straightforward ways to accomplish the project's objectives eliminate huge amounts of complexity and therefore huge numbers of errors. Most features can be implemented using a 2-hour, 2-day, 2-week, or 2-month approach. Developers should start with the 2-hour approach, which will tend to be the simplest, most straightforward, and least error-prone version. If that version has been implemented and still isn't sufficient, developers can implement the next simplest version—the 2-day version—to see whether that's sufficient to meet software requirements. These numbers shouldn't be taken literally; sometimes, the simplest version of a complex feature will take days or weeks. In any case, developers should make a practice of proceeding from simple to complex, not the opposite.

The French writer Voltaire commented that an essay was finished not when there was nothing more to add, but when there was nothing more to take away. The default movement on a software project should be in the direction of taking elements of the software away to make it simpler rather than adding elements to make it more complex.

Focus on Shipping Software

Effective development teams are single-minded in their pursuit of releasing their products. One of the ways in which Microsoft has been particularly effective is explicitly focusing on the act of *shipping software*. Developers who see a product through to release receive a "Ship-It" award, which acknowledges them for driving a product to completion. Developers who have been with the company for many years typically have large collections of Ship-It awards. This simple practice emphasizes to developers that Microsoft doesn't make its money by *developing* software; it makes its money by *shipping* software. That's how most other companies that produce software make their money, too.

A focus on releasing the software is just as important for business software developers who release software to their internal customers as it is for shrink-wrap developers who release software to the general public. A clear vision helps any kind of software development team focus on the product release goal. If developers carry different visions of the product they're developing to the end of the project, a great deal of time, effort, and money will go into reconciling the differences in their visions.

A clear architecture can also help align the development team with the release goal. The project team that doesn't create a good architecture will have difficulty focusing on technical work. The team that does create a good architecture will have built focus into the project at a deep technical level.

The software development team must be relentless in ensuring that every technical decision contributes toward satisfying the system's minimum required functions. If a project team is working on an academic project for a university class, there might be some reason to make a program arbitrarily more complicated. But if a team is working on a commercial product, its mission is to provide the simplest, cleanest solution that solves the business problem. Any decision that is counter to this mission should be rejected.

One message of this book is that software development is inherently a functional activity that serves practical objectives. It has strong aesthetic and scientific components, but it is not art or science. The effective software developer realizes that software projects do not exist primarily to provide the developer with a high-tech sandbox, and prioritizes his or her activities accordingly. The Microsoft experience shows that this orientation toward results can be cultivated in project teams. The developer who does not share this focus on the bottom line is a drag on the project and ultimately of little use to the organization.

Survival Check

- The project team creates a detailed written plan designed to eliminate potentially costly problems early in the project.

- The project emphasizes the importance of upstream work by holding a Planning Checkpoint Review and making a go/no go decision when the project is about 10 percent complete.

- The project practices active risk management.

- The project plan emphasizes visibility and control.

- The project plan involves real users early and throughout the project.

- The project is conducted in a productive environment, or the project plan assumes lower productivity.

- The project plan calls for a simple-to-complex approach rather than the reverse.

5 The Successful Project at a Glance

Software projects are processes of discovery and invention. One of the best ways to organize them is by using an approach called "staged delivery," in which the software's functionality is developed and delivered in stages, with the most important functionality delivered earliest. When a project is underway, many activities overlap, but these activities generally proceed from abstract to specific. Over the course of a project, source code tends to grow in an S-shape curve rather than linearly, and most of the code is generated during the middle third of the project. Tracking code growth provides insight into a project's status. Upper management, customers, and users can track well-run projects by keeping tabs on a clearly defined set of major milestones and deliverables.

This chapter describes what a successful project looks like from an altitude of 20,000 feet. It presents different views that provide insight into the flow, staffing, progression of activities, code growth, and major milestones and deliverables of a project.

INTELLECTUAL PHASES

Before discussing how software projects are divided into planning phases, I think it's useful to understand in a general way what happens as a project progresses from problem definition to software delivery.

Software projects are divided into three conceptual stages, as shown in Figure 5-1. During the early part of the project, the focus is on "discovery"—especially discovery of the user's real requirements. This first phase is characterized by converting areas of uncertainty into areas of certainty through technical investigation work such as interviewing users and building user interface prototypes.

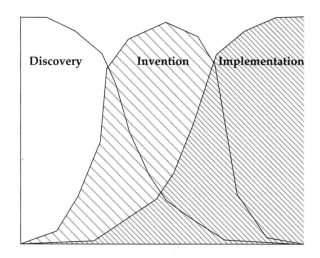

FIGURE 5-1   *Conceptual phases of a software project. The kind of work performed during each phase of the project varies, but each kind of work occurs to some extent throughout the project.*

In the middle of the project, the focus shifts to invention. At the macro level, developers invent a software architecture and design. At the micro level, each function or class may require small inventions.

Like the discovery phase, the invention phase is characterized by the transformation of uncertainties into certainties. If anything, uncertainty during invention is higher than during discovery—during discovery developers can be certain that the answer is "out there" somewhere. During invention, there can be no such assurance.

During the final part of the project, the focus shifts again, this time to implementation. Unlike the phases of discovery and invention, implementation involves much less uncertainty and focuses on realizing the potential that has been mapped out during discovery and invention.

As Figure 5-1 illustrates, discovery, invention, and implementation are each occurring to some degree throughout a software project. This is one reason that strictly phased planning approaches don't work very well. A project plan must allow discovery, invention, and implementation to coexist.

PROJECT FLOW

With some software development approaches, the project team completes large sections of the life cycle almost in secret. Technical projects often provide status reports such as "90 percent complete." That's not very encouraging to customers who have learned the hard way that if the first 90 percent of a project takes 90 percent of the time, the last 10 percent of the project can take another 90 percent of the time.

The project plan described in this book follows the general pattern known as "staged delivery." This plan provides for delivering software in successive stages throughout a project, rather than all at once at the end of the project. Figure 5-2 on the following page illustrates this approach.

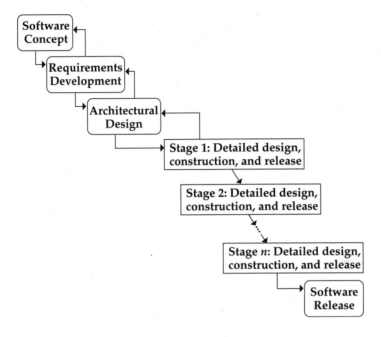

FIGURE 5-2   *Staged Delivery Plan. The project is first carefully defined and designed, and then functionality is delivered in successive stages.*

As you can see from the diagram, staged delivery emphasizes project planning and risk reduction. The project team develops a software concept first, then gathers and analyzes requirements, and then completes an architectural design. Work during each of these stages is driven by the goal of eliminating risks through active risk management and careful planning of the stages yet to come.

Within each implementation stage (shown as stages 1–n in the figure), the project team does detailed design, coding, debugging, and testing, creating a potentially releasable product at the end of each stage. The diagram shows three stages, but you can set up a project to use as many or as few stages as you want—some projects have only three or four stages and some have many more, delivering software as often as every week.

BENEFITS OF STAGED DELIVERY

Staged delivery provides several important benefits, which are described in the following sections.

Critical Functionality Is Available Earlier

The stages in a staged delivery project are typically designed to deliver the software's most important functionality first. Users who are waiting for particular functionality don't have to wait until the whole product is ready; they have to wait only until the first stage of the product is ready. In contrast to the ineffective free-for-all often found on rush projects, staged delivery can be a valuable approach on a project with a tight schedule.

Risks Are Reduced Early

This approach emphasizes planning and risk management throughout the project. Delivering the product in stages reduces the technical risk of unsuccessful integration because it forces integration to occur more often than it would if the software was delivered at the end of the project. It reduces requirements risk by putting usable software into end users' hands at the earliest possible moment. It reduces management risk by generating tangible signs of progress at frequent intervals. It reduces planning risk by building opportunities to revise plans into the end of each stage.

Problems Become Evident Early

When you plan to deliver releases early and often, you get early, frequent, indisputable progress reports. Either the release is done on time or it isn't. The work's quality is obvious from the release's quality. If the development team is in trouble, you discover that within the first one or two releases; you don't have to wait until the project is "90 percent complete" and still 0 percent functional.

Status-Reporting Overhead Is Reduced

Staged delivery also goes a long way toward eliminating the administrative time that developers spend creating progress reports and other traditional progress-tracking reports.

———◆———

The working software is a more accurate status report than any paper report could ever be.

———◆———

Staged Delivery Makes More Options Available

The fact that the project team has releasable software at the end of each stage doesn't mean that it actually has to release the software. But it can release the software if it wants to, and driving to a releasable state increases the chance that when the team does want to release software, it will have something that's ready. If you don't use staged delivery, you won't have an option.

Staged Delivery Reduces the Possibility of Estimation Error

Staged delivery sidesteps the problem of bad estimates by delivering early and often. Instead of making one large estimate for the whole project, the project team can make several smaller estimates for several smaller releases. With each release, it can learn from the mistakes in its estimates, recalibrate its approach, and improve the accuracy of future estimates—for both the current project and future projects.

Staged Delivery Balances Flexibility and Efficiency

Delivering software in stages gives the project team a defined set of time periods to consider making changes to the software—the time between stages. Addressing changes between stages frees the team from having to consider changes continuously and builds a guarantee into the project that changes will be considered periodically.

Costs of Staged Delivery

From the preceding list of benefits, it might sound as though staged delivery has no disadvantages, and that isn't quite true. Staged delivery has some noticeable costs. It increases project overhead because of the time needed to drive the software to a releasable stage multiple times, retest already-tested features in each stage, perform version control tasks associated with making a delivery, address the extra complexity of supporting additional versions of the software in the field (if the staged deliveries are actually released into the field), plan the staged releases themselves, and so on.

Some of these costs are not really extra—they are costs that often remain hidden until the end of a project but that are simply exposed earlier when staged delivery is used. Defect detection and correction fall into this category. People who work on a staged delivery project for the first time sometimes complain that they're spending all their time fixing defects. In reality, they're correcting defects they would have had to correct anyway. The difference is that the defects are detected earlier in the project and can be corrected closer to the time they were created, which makes them less expensive to fix.

Other costs truly are extra. The activities associated with actually releasing the software multiple times increases the overhead and total cost of the project.

———◆———

Staged delivery is not a panacea. But, on balance, the additional overhead it demands is a small price to pay for the significantly improved status visibility, quality visibility, flexibility, estimation accuracy, and risk reduction it provides.

———◆———

Planning Phases

The staged delivery diagram shown in Figure 5-2 implies that early project activities such as requirements analysis and architecture are performed one at a time. It's important to complete most of the requirements work before plunging into architecture, and it's important to complete most of the architecture work before beginning detailed design and implementation in earnest. But in reality these activities overlap, which is both inevitable and desirable. Figure 5-3 on the following page shows a typical overlap.

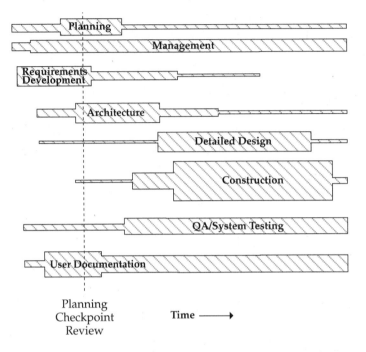

Planning
Checkpoint   Time ⟶
Review

FIGURE 5-3   *Typical activity overlap. Early activities of requirements development and architecture do not overlap as much as later activities of detailed design, coding, integration, and testing. Bar thickness indicates the relative staffing levels throughout the phases of a project.*

The figure suggests that many activities overlap to some extent over the life of a project, but in the early stages, one activity should be mostly complete before the next one begins. This approach is recommended because errors tend to become more expensive to fix over time. The 80/20 rule applies. Try to complete 80 percent of the requirements before beginning architecture and 80 percent of the architecture before beginning detailed design. Eighty percent is not a magic number, but it is a good rule of thumb: it allows the team to do most of the requirements work at the beginning of the project while implicitly acknowledging that it is not possible to do all of it.

Detailed design, coding, integration, and testing are all done at about the same time. This is because the staged delivery approach results in mini-cycles of design, coding, integration, and testing in each stage. User documentation is begun early because of the way requirements are developed (described in Chapter 8) and continues throughout the project. Management and planning are also performed throughout the project. The complexity of Figure 5-3 might suggest that this breakdown applies only to large projects, but in practice virtually all projects perform these generic functions, just to greater or lesser degrees.

STAFF BUILDUP

From a staffing point of view, two general phases exist in a well-run staged delivery project: software definition and staged delivery. During the first phase, the software is being defined: the team is developing requirements and constructing the software architecture. The overall level of effort during this phase is considerably lower than it is during the main implementation phase. During this stage, the 10 to 20 percent go/no go decision will be made. The people doing this work should be highly skilled senior developers.

The second major phase is staged delivery. During this phase, the project team is doing the detailed design, construction, and software testing. Highly skilled senior developers play a role during this phase too, but a project also needs quality assurance staff, technical writers, and less experienced developers.

During the final 50 percent or so of the project, you can see that the level of effort for quality assurance, detailed design, and coding stay relatively flat. In all-at-once development approaches, projects typically have to staff up in the middle of the project and then staff down toward the end of the project. Staged delivery projects can use a relatively flat staffing model for most of the project, which smoothes out cash flow, hiring, training, testing, and use of computing resources.

The view of the activities shown in Figure 5-3 doesn't really indicate how much total time is devoted to each activity. Figure 5-4 shows a typical distribution of effort across activities on a project.

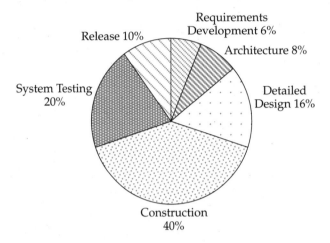

FIGURE 5-4   *Activity distribution by percent of effort consumed.*

Note that Figure 5-4's "release" activity isn't shown separately on Figure 5-3. Release activity includes all end-of-project tasks such as getting the release approved by all the project's stakeholders, creating the final project log, and creating the project history report.

The specific numbers shown in this chart are rules of thumb and should not be taken too literally, but they do provide a few insights. The upstream activities of requirements development and architecture consume a relatively small portion of the project's effort; the downstream activities of construction and system testing consume more. Upstream activities exert a great deal of leverage over the downstream activities, however, so it is at least as critical that upstream activities be done well and that downstream activities be done well.

To round out the project picture, Figure 5-5 shows a typical distribution of schedule across a project's activities.

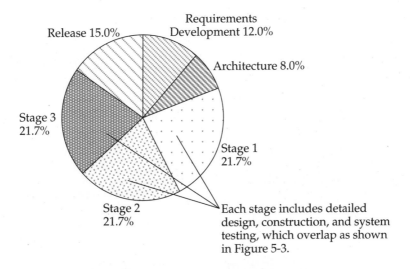

FIGURE 5-5 *Activity distribution by percent of schedule consumed, assuming a project is divided into three stages. (Numbers do not add to 100 percent due to rounding error.) Compare this figure to Figure 5-4: schedule and effort on a software project are not distributed in exactly the same way.*

A key insight to be gained from these figures is that the percentage of a project's *schedule* devoted to an activity is not the same as the percentage of a project's *effort* devoted to the activity. Requirements development typically consumes 12 percent of a project's schedule, but only 6 percent of its effort. Because the upstream activities tend to be less tangible and require deeper contemplation, they must proceed at a slower pace than downstream activities.

CODE GROWTH CURVE

The previous figures are meant to convey the idea that a lot of the work performed early in a project does not produce any code. Indeed, code tends to be produced slowly, if at all, during the first third of a project. The first third of the project is devoted to understanding requirements in detail and developing a high-quality architecture so that the project team can "measure twice and cut once." The middle third of the project is focused on building the project, and during this period code is generated rapidly. The final third of the project focuses on verifying that code written in the middle third is good enough to turn over to users. This period focuses on defect corrections and carefully controlled additions to the code base. As in the first third, code is added slowly. Figure 5-6 illustrates a well-run project's code-growth pattern.

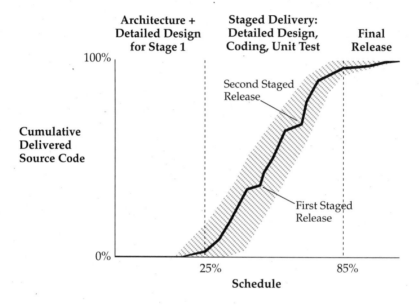

FIGURE 5-6 *Typical code growth pattern on a project. Most code growth occurs during the middle third of the project.*

The black line shows the nominal code growth pattern, and the shaded area shows the range of normal variations. The variations in code growth in the middle of the project are due to interim releases in which the project's emphasis shifts from generating new code to raising the quality of existing code. The project shown in Figure 5-6 had two interim releases before its final release.

Once you understand this code growth pattern, you have a powerful tool to use to assess project status. Well-run projects keep track of the code that is being integrated into the project each week. If the amount of new code being added has almost stopped, the project may be about ready to release. But if new code is still being added at a fast clip, the project is still in the middle third and is not yet close to release.

Similarly, if developers are adding a lot of code before they have completed architecture, you're almost guaranteed to have a long stay in system testing while developers repair all the errors they introduced by developing source code before the design was strong enough to support it.

One serious error that some projects make is releasing the product at the 85 percent mark instead of waiting until the 100 percent mark. If project leaders don't understand the software development pattern described in Figure 5-6, they might assume that their software is ready to release as soon as the new code development begins to taper off—especially when the project is under significant schedule pressure. Unfortunately, a decision to release at the 85 percent point means the software has not spent enough time in the final quality assurance phase, which essentially amounts to a decision to release low-quality software.

MAJOR MILESTONES AND DELIVERABLES

At some point the general patterns described in the last few sections need to be nailed down to a detailed list of milestones and deliverables. Major milestones are used to track the project's progress at the highest level. Figure 5-7 on the following page summarizes the top-level phases and milestones for the plan this book describes.

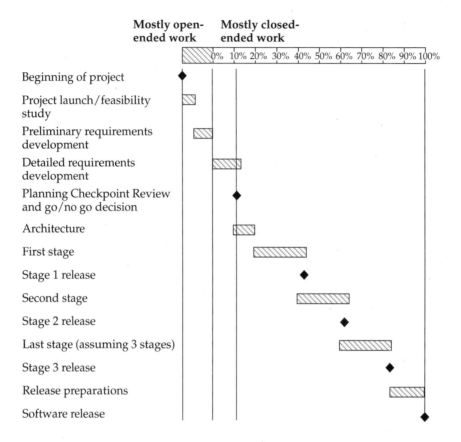

FIGURE 5-7   *Top-level project phases and milestones. A well-run software project can follow this general plan regardless of its size.*

This general project outline applies to virtually any size project. In practice, preliminary work in each phase often begins earlier than shown in the figure, and follow-up work extends later than shown in the figure. The figure illustrates the times during which major emphasis is placed on each activity. (Figure 5-3 shows the overlap more fully.)

Upper managers and customers are sometimes frustrated that milestones on a software project are too intangible to function as reliable status indicators, but if you follow the practices recommended in this book, tracking progress against milestones will provide good insight into the project's status. Table 5-1 lists more detailed milestones and activities that correspond to Figure 5-7's top-level milestones and activities.

TABLE 5-1   TOP-LEVEL MILESTONES AND DELIVERABLES[*]

◆ *Beginning of project*

☐ Key project decision-maker identified

☐ Vision statement created, reviewed, and baselined

☐ Business case for the software established

☐ Preliminary effort and schedule targets created, reviewed, and baselined

☐ Team of 2–3 senior developers on board

☐ Change Control Plan created, reviewed, and baselined

☐ Initial Top 10 Risks List created, reviewed, and baselined

☐ Software Project Log started

The work done during this part of the project is open-ended. It includes, among other things, coming to an understanding of just how large the project is. Consequently, the schedule and effort involved in this part vary greatly from project to project.

◆ *Project launch/feasibility study complete*

☐ QA lead on board

☐ Documentation lead on board

☐ Key users identified and interviewed

☐ Simple user-interface prototype created, reviewed by users until acceptable, and baselined

☐ User Interface Style Guide created, reviewed, and baselined

☐ First project estimates (accurate to +100%, −50%) created, reviewed, and baselined

☐ Preliminary Software Development Plan created, reviewed, and baselined

☐ Top 10 Risks List updated

☐ Software Project Log updated

The work in this part of the project is also open-ended and varies from project to project.

◆ *Preliminary requirements development complete*

(continued)

*This table is available in electronic form on the *Survival Guide* Web site.

At this point, the open-ended work on the project has been completed. Now a little more work is needed to support making a go/no go decision about the project.

☐ Detailed user-interface prototype created, reviewed, and baselined

☐ User Manual/Requirements Specification created, reviewed, and baselined

☐ Software Quality Assurance Plan created, reviewed, and baselined

☐ Detailed Software Development Plan created, reviewed, and baselined

☐ Project estimates updated (accurate to +75%, −45%)

☐ Top 10 Risks List updated

☐ Software Project Log updated

At this point, about 12 percent of the project-lifetime schedule and 6 percent of the effort have been expended. These percentages do not include the work done on the project launch/feasibility study and preliminary requirements development.

◆ **Detailed requirements development complete**
◆ **Planning Checkpoint Review and go/no go decision**

☐ Most of development team on board

☐ Most of QA staff on board

☐ Documentation staff reduced after completing User Manual/ Requirements Specification (unless other significant documentation products will be produced)

☐ Software Architecture document created, reviewed, and baselined

☐ Software Integration Procedure created, reviewed, and baselined

☐ Staged Delivery Plan created, reviewed, and baselined

☐ Software test cases for Stage 1 created, reviewed, and baselined

☐ User Manual/Requirements Specification updated

☐ Project estimates updated (accurate to +40%, −30%)

☐ Top 10 Risks List updated

☐ Software Development Plan updated

☐ Software Project Log updated

At this point, about 20 percent of the project-lifetime schedule and 14 percent of the effort have been expended.

◆ **Architecture complete**

☐ Full development team on board

☐ Full QA staff on board

☐ Beginning-of-stage planning completed

☐ Detailed Design Document for Stage 1 created, reviewed, and baselined

☐ Detailed Software Construction Plan for Stage 1 including miniature milestones created, reviewed, and baselined

☐ Software test cases for next stage created, reviewed, and baselined

☐ Software test cases for Stage 1 updated

☐ Software build instructions (make files) for Stage 1 created

☐ Software source code for Stage 1 created, reviewed, and baselined

☐ Install program created, reviewed, and baselined

☐ User Manual/Requirements Specification updated

☐ Stage 1 "feature-complete" product delivered

☐ Project estimates updated (accurate to +30%, −20%)

☐ Top 10 Risks List updated

☐ Software Project Log updated

At this point, about 45 percent of the project-lifetime schedule and 40 percent of the effort have been expended, assuming the project has 3 stages.

◆   **First stage code complete**

☐ Same activities as above

At this point, about 65 percent of the project-lifetime schedule and 65 percent of the effort have been expended.

◆   **Second stage code complete**

☐ Detailed Design Document for last stage created, reviewed, and baselined

☐ Software test cases for all stages updated

☐ Software source code for all stages updated

☐ Software build instructions (make files) for all stages updated

(continued)

☐ Install program updated

☐ If software is a business system, deployment document (cutover handbook) complete; user training complete; and deployment team ready

☐ Integrated "feature-complete" product delivered

☐ Project estimates updated (accurate to +5%, −5%)

☐ Top 10 Risks List updated

☐ Software Project Log updated

At this point, about 85 percent of the project-lifetime schedule and 90 percent of the effort have been expended.

◆ **Last stage code complete (third stage, if three stages are used)**

☐ Release checklist created, reviewed, and baselined

☐ Release Sign-Off Form signed by all parties and put under change control

☐ Functionally correct product delivered

☐ Functionally correct install program delivered

☐ Final test cases delivered

☐ Software duplication media ("gold disks") delivered

☐ Project archival media (source code, build environment, etc.) stored offsite

☐ Final Software Project Log updated

☐ Project History document created, reviewed, and baselined

At this point, 100 percent of the project-lifetime schedule and effort have been expended.

◆ **Product release**

Sometimes people wonder why software projects take so long. The list of deliverables in Table 5-1 helps to answer that question. Each deliverable represents a significant amount of work that must be accomplished for the project to proceed efficiently.

———◆———

*Most poorly run projects ultimately perform all
the tasks listed in Table 5-1. But because their
tasks are poorly coordinated and inefficiently
executed, poorly run projects ultimately
expend more effort for less benefit.*

———◆———

One of the reasons people resist "processes" is because at the beginning of a process-oriented project, they see a list like this and think, "The project is going to take forever if we do all that stuff!" The reality is that if a project doesn't do all that stuff, it will take even longer. Even small projects need to perform virtually all of the tasks listed in Table 5-1, though some of the tasks will take little time to complete. We might wish that there weren't so much work required, but with software projects, ignorance is hardly ever bliss, and project stakeholders will all be better off if they recognize from the beginning what work is needed.

Survival Check

 The project uses a staged delivery approach.

 Upper management, the customer, or both track progress by following the code growth curve.

 Upper management, the customer, or both track progress by keeping tabs on major milestones and deliverables.

II

SURVIVAL PREPARATIONS

6 Hitting a Moving Target

Effective projects control changes; ineffective projects allow changes to control them. Keys to successful change control include establishing a change board, limiting major changes to predefined points in the project, and placing major work products under change control.

Y ou can most easily hit a target if you know precisely when the target is going to move and when it is going to stop—you save your energy while the target is moving, and take aim when it stops. Because of changing markets and evolving technology, software project feature sets amount to moving targets. Some movement is inevitable; other movement can be controlled. Projects that do not actively control changes to their feature sets—that try to hit moving targets—expose themselves to significant and in many cases insurmountable risk. Controlling changes as an integral part of project planning is critical to project success. As Gene Forte says, "change control" is in marked contrast to "change surrender."

———◆———

Change control allows all necessary changes to be made while ensuring that change impacts are understood projectwide.

———◆———

CHANGE CONTROL PROCEDURE

At the most basic level, change control addresses changes to requirements and source code. More advanced projects integrate change control throughout the project's activities (project plans, estimates, requirements, architecture, detailed design, source code, test plans, and documentation). Formally speaking, "change control" is the practice of evaluating, controlling, and approving important changes made during the project and of ensuring that all project stakeholders are aware of the changes that affect them. The basic change control procedure involves the following steps:

1. The initial development work for a work product (such as the project requirements) is performed without change control coming into play. During this period, changes can be made freely to the work product.

2. The work product is subjected to a technical review, which determines whether initial development work on it can be declared complete.

3. When initial development is complete, the work product is submitted to a "change board." The change board typically consists of representatives from each of the project's major concerned

parties, for example, project management, marketing, development, quality assurance, documentation, and user support. (This board also goes by the name of "War Council," "Change Czar," and similar names, depending on whether the project team fancies itself an executive committee, military junta, or Russian nobility.) On small projects, the change board might consist of only one, two, or three members. On the largest projects involving multiple companies, it can swell to 30 or more. Its most important objective is to serve as a central clearinghouse for changes to ensure that all important viewpoints are considered.

When a work product is submitted to the change board, it is baselined. At this point, any further changes to the work product are subject to a more systematic change process than was used during Step 1.

4. The work product is placed under "revision control." Revision control refers to a software revision control program (also known as "version control" or "source code control") that is capable of archiving multiple versions of anything stored electronically. Although most commonly used for source code, most revision control systems will archive anything that can be stored in electronic form—documents, project plans, spreadsheets, design diagrams, source code, test cases, and so on.

5. Further changes to the work product are treated systematically:

    a. Changes are proposed via Change Proposals. A Change Proposal describes the work product in question, the proposed change, and the impact of the change (both cost and benefit) from the point of view of the party proposing the change. Creating a Change Proposal is a good idea on even the smallest projects because it provides a record of the project's decisions that is far more reliable than people's memories.

    b. The change board identifies parties that might be affected by the change and distributes the Change Proposal for their review.

    c. The concerned parties each assess the costs and benefits of the proposed change from their individual viewpoints.

    d.   The change board members combine their assessments and prioritize the Change Proposal—either they accept it, reject it, or defer it to a later time.

    e.   The change board notifies all concerned parties about how the Change Proposal was resolved.

I've described this process somewhat formally, which might make it seem bureaucratic. But if you read the description of each step carefully, you will see that the steps are really just formalized common sense: assess change impacts before making changes, allow affected parties to review the proposed changes, and notify affected parties of changes once they have been approved. What is the alternative to this? Don't assess impacts before making changes? Don't allow affected parties to review changes before they are made? Don't notify affected parties of approved changes? It sounds ridiculous, but that is exactly what happens on projects that don't use systematic change control.

CHANGE CONTROL BENEFITS

Change control produces several significant benefits. Its primary benefit is that it does what it's intended to do—it protects the project from unnecessary changes by ensuring that Change Proposals are considered systematically. The addition of unnecessary features is traditionally one of the most serious software development risks because of the related increases in software complexity, destabilizing effect on design and code, and increased cost and schedule associated with expanding the product concept.

Change control improves the quality of decisions made about the software by ensuring that all concerned parties are involved in decisions. Similarly, it improves the visibility of necessary changes by ensuring that concerned parties are notified when changes are being considered and when they are resolved. That in turn improves the project team's ability to track progress.

Change control combats "mushy milestones." One of the more subtle risks on a software project is that the project team will reach a milestone and declare that milestone to have been met even though the team's work doesn't really satisfy the milestone criteria. The project team might not have created a really complete architecture document, but when the milestone date for architecture arrives, it'll simply declare whatever it has completed up to that point to be the architecture—especially if its under pressure to meet an ambitious delivery date.

Under the change control process, the architecture (or any other work product) must be reviewed, signed off, and placed under change control before it can be considered complete. It's a lot harder to slip a mushy architecture past the architecture milestone when all the concerned parties have to sign off on the architecture document and when they know that any further changes to it will have to go through the systematic change control process.

This elimination of mushy milestones also improves status visibility. If you know that milestones are *hard*, the fact that the project has completed a milestone is a meaningful status indicator.

Basically, change control increases accountability. Concerned parties have to sign off on work products before they are baselined. People who propose changes to baselined work products have to justify why they want changes, and their reasons become part of the permanent record of the project. People who resist the changes have to explain why they don't want them, and those reasons also become part of the project's permanent record. One of the common denominators of projects that are in trouble is a lack of accountability.

——————◆——————

*On successful projects, project members actively
seek accountability both for their own work and for
other work that affects them.*

——————◆——————

BENEFITS OF AUTOMATED REVISION CONTROL

A corollary benefit of change control is versioning. Automated revision control software enables project members to easily retrieve any version of any major document that has been produced on the project. They can retrieve initial project plans, revised project plans, and current project plans. They can re-create any version of the product that has ever been released to a customer. With change control, they will have a detailed historical record of the project and will be able to retrace the development of estimates, prototypes, designs, and source code over the course of the project.

An automated revision control system makes all project documents publicly available at all times. Any person who needs to examine the project plan, requirements, designs, coding standards, user interface prototype, or other work product can retrieve that work product from the revision control system. There is no danger of losing these work products or of being unable to get a copy when needed. Getting a current copy of a document does not depend on being able to find the person who "owns" that document. Although this might seem to be a minor benefit, few software personnel who have worked on projects that make project materials so readily available ever want to work on projects that don't.

Most revision control software can also produce summary information that's useful in assessing project status. It can produce statistics about the number of lines of code added to, changed in, or deleted from the project each week.

COMMON CHANGE CONTROL ISSUES

Organizations implementing change control for the first time typically have questions about how to handle a few common issues.

HOW TO CONSIDER CHANGES

The change control board will typically consider the following factors when it decides how to resolve a proposed change:

- What is the expected benefit of the change?

- How would the change affect the project's cost?

- How would the change affect the project's schedule?

- How would the change affect the software's quality?

- How would the change affect the project's resource allocation? Would it add work to people already on the project's critical path?

- Can the change be deferred to a later stage of the project or a later version of the software?

- Is the project at a point when making the change would risk destabilizing the software?

WHEN TO CONSIDER CHANGES

The change board meets as needed—typically biweekly in the early stages of a project, between stages in the middle of the project, and more often as the project approaches its release date. The change board can approve changes at any time during the project but should generally try to limit the number of times that project personnel will be asked to evaluate change impacts. Early in the project—during requirements development and architecture—changes can be considered as they arise. Later in the project, the development team should not be subjected to a continuous barrage of change requests; it should be subjected only to a few barrages of change requests. Part of the change board's job is to act as a buffer between the development team and the people requesting changes so that the development team isn't continuously distracted from its work by evaluating change impacts. In the later phases of a project, the change board should collect proposed changes for consideration in batches. In a staged delivery approach, the times between stages are ideal for considering batches of changes.

To a large extent, how often changes are considered depends on the personalities of the development team, customer, manager, and other project stakeholders. If stakeholders place a premium on orderly, efficient operation, they will typically want to consider changes less frequently. If they place a greater premium on quick resolution of outstanding issues, they'll want to consider them more frequently.

HOW TO HANDLE SMALL CHANGES

The change board should use common sense in establishing streamlined procedures for categories of changes that do not have far-reaching impacts, such as minor defect corrections. Those changes can be considered and accepted *en masse* by the change control board, or the change control plan can automatically approve them. For example, the change control plan might automatically approve fixes for errors that crash the system or errors that affect the accuracy of a software's calculations.

How to Handle Political Issues

For people who have not worked with a formal change control process, the process will seem cumbersome at first. After project members become familiar with it, however, it requires little time compared to the benefit it provides. For small changes, the change impact can often be assessed during the change board meeting itself, and the time required to complete Steps 5a–5e may be only a few minutes or less.

One initial effect of implementing change control is that fewer changes will be accepted than were accepted previously. Some people will feel that getting any changes accepted at all is impossible. Although the change board might initially seem to be miring the project in bureaucracy, it is always free to approve as many changes as it wants. Before change control, change impacts are usually not fully considered; once they are fully considered, fewer changes will be judged valuable enough to approve. This sometimes uncomfortable period marks an important transition from letting changes control a project to making the project control changes.

Some of the loudest objections to change control will come from the people who have been most successful at ramrodding changes through without giving the project team enough time to consider the full impacts of those changes. With change control in place, those people will not be successful as often as they were previously. One of change control's benefits is its ability to rein in hastily considered changes.

——◆——

People who are used to getting their way can still get their way with systematic change control, but they'll have to do it through a process that emphasizes visible decision making and accountability.

——◆——

Development personnel need to realize that this will be a difficult transition for some people to make and should prepare for it.

Which Work Products to Place Under Change Control

The change control plan should include a list of the work products that will be placed under change control. At a minimum, this list should include the work products listed in Table 6-1.

TABLE 6-1 **WORK PRODUCTS**
PLACED UNDER CHANGE CONTROL

Work Product
Change Control Plan
Change Proposals
Vision statement
Top 10 Risks List
Software Development Plan, including project cost and schedule estimates
User Interface Prototype
User Interface Style Guide
User Manual/Requirements Specification
Quality Assurance Plan
Software Architecture
Software Integration Procedure
Staged Delivery Plan
Individual Stage Plans, including miniature milestone schedules
Coding Standard
Software test cases
Source code
Media incorporated into the product, including graphics, sound, video, and so on
Software build instructions (make files)
Detailed Design Document for each stage
Software Construction Plan for each stage
Install program
Deployment Document (Cutover Handbook)
Release Checklist
Release Sign-Off Form
Software Project Log
Software Project History Document

Each of the work products is initially placed under change control at the time it is "baselined." (See Table 5-1, "Top-Level Milestones and Deliverables" on page 65.)

This list of work products represents a healthy minimum set of deliverables to place under change control. When you see a set of work products like this list, you might think, "That's a lot of overhead and extra work."

Creating these products *is* overhead and extra work—it probably adds a few percentage points of overhead to the project. But there is no way to provide the status visibility, risk reduction, and project control—in short, the greatly increased chance of project success—without creating and controlling work products more or less like these. Because of the significant benefit they provide, in most business situations, the decision to accept this particular kind of overhead is not just a good trade-off—it's an excellent one.

For any one project, creating all these work products the first time will be a lot of work. On the second or third project, however, the development team can create many of them simply by modifying previous versions of similar work products.[1]

COMMITTING TO CHANGE CONTROL

For change control to work, the project and the organization of which the project is a part must commit to change control. This commitment needs to take place on several levels.

Software change control activities need to be planned. The change control plan procedure and list of work products described in this chapter should be expressed within a written Change Control Plan. The Software Development Plan (discussed in the next chapter) should reference the Change Control Plan as part of the official software development process.

Project members must be given time to carry out their change control responsibilities. At a minimum, each project member will spend some time assessing the impact of a few proposed changes. A few project members will also spend time attending change board meetings.

The organization must accept the decisions of the change board at all levels. Change control will be next to meaningless if the project manager or marketing department can summarily override change board decisions, or if software developers add changes to the software without honoring the change control procedure.

---

1. Samples of some of these documents can be found on the *Survival Guide* Web site.

Survival Check

 The project has a change board.

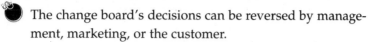 The change board's decisions can be reversed by management, marketing, or the customer.

 The project has a written, approved Change Control Plan.

Project team members aren't given enough time to carry out the plan.

Work products aren't actually put under change control.

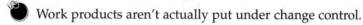 Change Proposals are evaluated by all the project's concerned parties before they are resolved.

The change board notifies the project's concerned parties of how each Change Proposal is resolved.

The change board has the project team evaluate changes in batches so that the team is not distracted by a constant barrage of change requests.

7
Preliminary Planning

Successful projects begin planning early. Preliminary planning activities include defining a project vision, identifying an executive sponsor, setting targets for project scope, managing risks, and mapping out strategies for using personnel effectively. These preliminary plans are captured in a Software Development Plan.

You might think that not much can be done to plan a project before its requirements are known. On the contrary, preparing preliminary plans before plunging into requirements development is both useful and important. The following topics should be addressed in the preliminary Software Development Plan, which is described at the end of the chapter:

◆ Project vision

◆ Executive sponsorship

◆ Project scope targets

◆ Publicizing plans and progress

◆ Risk management

◆ Personnel strategies

◆ Time accounting

A discussion of the topics themselves constitutes most of this chapter.

PROJECT VISION

Before the project gets rolling, a team needs to buy in to a common vision. Without such a shared vision, high-performance teamwork cannot take place. A study of 75 teams found that in *every case* in which the team functioned effectively, the team had a clear understanding of its objective.

Sharing a vision is useful on several levels. Agreement about the project vision helps to streamline decision making on smaller issues. It also helps to keep the team focused and avoid time-wasting side trips. A common vision builds trust among the team members because they know that they are all working toward the same objective. The team can make decisions and then execute them without squabbling and without revisiting issues that have already been decided. An effective team builds a level of cooperation that allows them to outperform a mere collection of individuals with similar skills.

An effective vision can have a motivating effect, and to do that, it needs to be elevating. The team needs to be presented with a challenge, a mission. Teams don't form around mundane goals: "We'd like to create the third-best Internet Web site designer on the market and deliver it 25 percent later than the industry average." That is not a compelling vision.

The response to challenge is emotional, and it is influenced as much by the way the work is assigned or described as by the work itself. Here's a restatement of the ho-hum goal: "We're going to create an Internet Web site designer that will take us from 0 market share to 25 percent market share in its first 6 months. We're cash-poor, so we're going to make it our goal to define a feature set and ship date that will allow us to use a small, sharp, highly efficient team in order to establish a foothold in the market before we run out of cash." A team might very well form around that restated vision.

Elevating though it must be, the vision statement must also be *achievable*. Sales and marketing personnel can be motivated by impossible goals, but software developers tend to see them as illogical and often find them demotivating. The same applies to sets of goals in which each goal individually is achievable but the set of goals, in combination, is unachievable: the goals of short schedule, low cost, or rich functionality might be achievable individually, but they usually cannot all be achieved simultaneously. Such sets of goals are seen by most developers as manipulative, and they won't work to them.

On some projects, you can't tell at the beginning of the project whether a set of goals is achievable. A common and damaging dynamic occurs when the development team begins to realize its goals are unachievable before management does. If management continues to insist that the goals are achievable after the team has figured out that they are not, team motivation and morale can sink fast. If you're a software project manager, be responsive when developers begin telling you that the project's goals are collectively unrealistic.

DEFINING WHAT TO LEAVE OUT

The vision statement should make it easy to determine what should go into the software *and what should not*. A vision statement such as "Create the world's best word processor" might be motivating, but it will not provide much guidance to the development team other than telling them to throw every conceivable feature into the software. The development of Microsoft Word for Windows 1.0 was hobbled by this kind of all-inclusive vision statement. That product ultimately took five years to develop, which was four years longer than originally planned. Alternatively, a vision statement such as "Create the world's easiest-to-use word processor" provides just as elevating a mission for the team to form around but provides much better guidance about what features to exclude.

———◆———

Creating wording that excludes at least as much as it includes is the hard part of writing a vision statement, but that wording is essential to the statement's usefulness.

———◆———

A good, exclusive vision statement helps the project team achieve the goal of software minimalism, which is essential for keeping project risk to a manageable level.

Committing to the Vision

The vision should be formalized in a written vision statement—when team members commit, there must be something for them to commit to. This vision statement then becomes the first item placed under change control. A vision statement can't provide top-level guidance if it changes haphazardly over the course of a project. It can and should be allowed to change in a controlled way as everyone's understanding of the developing software matures. Over time, your collection of vision statements from different projects will become an important resource for new projects, especially if you have classified these statements as effective and ineffective.

Executive Sponsorship

Executive sponsorship is the support given to the person or group who has final authority over projectwide decisions. Many surveys have identified effective executive sponsorship as critical to project success. For this reason, a project plan should identify the executive sponsor. This person or group should be responsible for committing to a feature set, approving the user interface design, and deciding whether the software is ready to release to its users or customers. If the decision-making authority is a group, each person in the group should represent a different interest—management, marketing, development, quality assurance, and so on. Sometimes this group is the change control board described in Chapter 6, "Hitting a Moving Target."

Early in my career I worked on a project for which I had five equal bosses. This set of bosses redirected my work so frequently and in so many ways that it took me two years to complete a one-year project. I felt like a piece of Silly Putty being pulled in five different directions, and our software ended up looking like a Silly Putty picture that had been stretched five different ways. Be sure that decisions come from one place, whether that one place is a single person or a single change control board. A single, clear decision-making authority is essential to an effectively functioning project.

PROJECT SCOPE TARGETS

Before much work has been done on the project, you should have an idea about the intended budget, schedule, staffing, and feature set of the software. This idea is not an estimate but a tentative target.

As the project progresses, the project team will gain insight about how much work will be needed to create the envisioned software, and as this awareness develops, any of several possibilities can arise:

◆   You find the initial project budget and schedule targets to be in close alignment with the envisioned feature set.

◆   You find the initial project budget and schedule targets to be insufficient to support the desired feature set, and you adjust the budget and schedule targets upward to support the desired feature set.

◆   You find the initial project budget and schedule targets to be insufficient to support the desired feature set, and you shrink the feature set to conform to the desired budget and schedule.

As I explained in conjunction with Figure 3-6 (on page 31), software development is a process of continual refinement in which more is learned about the technical extent of the software in each stage. Well-run projects invariably involve some give and take between feature set, budget, and schedule.

———◆———

*The best organizations plan to reestimate regularly
throughout a project and periodically adjust their
project plans based on the reestimation.*

———◆———

One of the most successful software organizations in the world, NASA's Software Engineering Laboratory (SEL), creates an initial project estimate after requirements have been defined and then refines that estimate five times over the course of a project at the estimation points that are shown in Table 7-1. At each estimation point, the development team makes a base estimate of the work remaining on the project. The range of uncertainty in the estimate is then expressed by taking the base estimate and multiplying it by Table 7-1's "upper limit" and "lower limit" numbers. In addition, the SEL's *Manager's Handbook* advises that the base estimates typically grow by 40 percent over the course of a project. (This dynamic was illustrated in Figure 3-6 on page 31.)

TABLE 7-1   **EFFORT ESTIMATE REFINEMENT
THROUGHOUT A PROJECT**

Estimation Point	Upper Limit	Lower Limit
End of requirements definition and specification	× 2.0	× 0.50
End of requirements analysis	× 1.75	× 0.57
End of preliminary design	× 1.4	× 0.71
End of detailed design	× 1.25	× 0.80
End of implementation	× 1.10	× 0.91
End of system testing	× 1.05	× 0.95

Considering the amount of uncertainty contained in the project estimates even after requirements development has been completed, the best way to think of preliminary schedule and budget targets created at software concept time is as aids that help the development team identify features that cannot be delivered within the desired targets. Eliminating these features from consideration early in the project helps to keep the project small, which addresses the major project risks of excessive complexity and gold-plating.

More detailed estimates are created later in the project and are explained in greater detail in Chapter 11, "Final Preparations."

PUBLICIZING PLANS AND PROGRESS

One common characteristic of unsuccessful software projects is that planning is conducted in secret. Usually, none of the planners intends to keep planning a secret, but none of them tries very hard to involve the rest of the project personnel either. The effect is virtually inevitable: plans created without the involvement of the developers, testers, and documentation staff who will actually perform the work do not address all necessary considerations, and the plans cannot be carried out. Because the plans cannot be followed, the project team ignores them and essentially runs free-form—that is, it runs out of control.

Project plans should be reviewed *and approved* by the people who will carry them out. Am I serious that the plans created by a manager have to be approved by the people that manager manages? Absolutely. The project plans will in fact be approved or disapproved by the project team once the project is under way, in the form of the many decisions they make about how to follow the plans and *whether* to follow them. If the project team doesn't approve of the project plans, the plans will not in fact be followed.

The effective software project manager acts as an orchestra conductor, as the person who coordinates the work of the team. The manager does not have perfect knowledge of the work required to carry out each aspect of the project, so it is necessary to incorporate input from each of the project's participants.

A software project cannot thrive when there is an adversarial relationship between project management and the project team. The manager shouldn't try to trick or goad the development team into doing its work. The team wants to do its work. What the team needs from project management is effective coordination of activities so that its efforts aren't wasted. The smart project manager makes sure the plans are approved by the project team before the bulk of the work gets under way.

————◆————

On a healthy project, all of the planning materials
are made available for public review—productivity
assumptions, schedules, schedule padding, risks,
task assignments, and any other planning
component.

————◆————

PUBLICIZING PROGRESS INDICATORS

Once the plan has been reviewed, approved, and put under change control, the core indicators of project health or dysfunction should be made visible to the entire project. The goal is to make basic project status readily available to all project stakeholders. This list of indicators includes at least the following information:

◆   List of tasks completed

◆   Defect statistics

◆   Top 10 Risks List

◆   Percent of schedule used

◆   Percent of resources used

◆   Project management's status reports to upper management

One way to achieve status visibility is to create a project intranet home page that contains pointers to general project information including project planning and tracking details, technical work products, and project deliverables. Figure 7-1 shows an example of such a Web page. Making these materials available on a Web site extends one step further Chapter 6's idea of using the revision control system to make all project materials available. On an intranet Web site, you can get current information about the project without knowing how to use the project's revision control system.

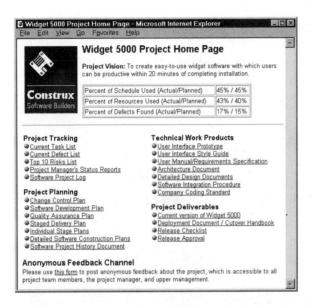

FIGURE 7-1   *Example of a software project intranet Web page containing up-to-date status, planning information, and key project work products.*

———◆———

There are no secrets on a successful software project. Both good and bad news must be able to move up and down the project hierarchy without restriction.

———◆———

RISK MANAGEMENT

One dictionary definition of "risk" is "possibility of loss or injury." Software development is an activity that involves the possibility of risk, or loss—in the form of budget and schedule overruns—no matter how it's conducted. But the way that software projects are typically conducted offers little chance of success at all, and that level of risk is completely unnecessary. As Figure 7-2 on the next page illustrates, I have found that the average project devotes virtually none of its efforts to reducing risk and consequently accepts unnecessarily high risk exposure.

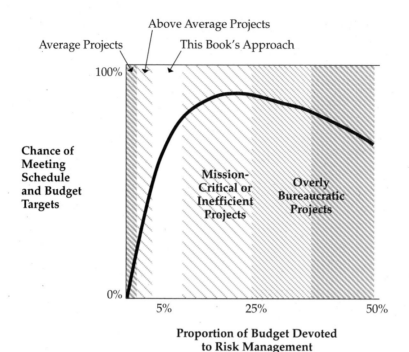

FIGURE 7-2   *Variation in risk level according to risk-management overhead. The average project devotes virtually no attention to risk management and accepts extremely high levels of risk as a consequence. Successful projects devote a small amount of overhead to risk management and substantially reduce their risk exposure.*

Devoting a small amount of attention to risk management produces dramatic benefits. In this book's approach, about 5 percent of the project's effort goes into activities that could be loosely categorized as "risk management." This small expenditure provides a dramatically improved chance of meeting schedule and budget targets. This book's approach should give most projects a 50 to 75 percent chance of being completed on time and within budget.

◆

Successful organizations actively look for ways to trade small amounts of increased overhead for large amounts of risk reduction.

◆

Some projects need to reduce risk even further, and to accomplish that, they are forced into the area of diminishing returns, shown in the lightly shaded area on the right in Figure 7-2. Still other projects, such as the historically paperwork-bound U.S. Department of Defense projects, are to the far right of the graph, devoting large percentages of their budgets in an attempt to assure on-time completion.

Because software development is inherently risky, most medium to large projects cannot attain a 100 percent chance of meeting schedule and budget targets without building in lavish safety margins. At some level of overhead (shown approximately in the graph), the overhead itself becomes a risk to the project and reduces the chance of meeting the project's schedule and budget targets.

COMMITTING TO RISK MANAGEMENT

Success at risk management depends on making the commitment to perform risk management, developing an ability to perform it, carrying out activities to perform it, and verifying that the management plan for each risk has been effective. If any of these important elements is missing, risk management will be ineffective.

A commitment to risk management consists of three elements. First, the project plan must describe a risk-management approach, such as the one described here, in writing. Second, the budget for the project must include funds earmarked for risk resolution. If no funds can be earmarked for risk resolution, the project cannot be considered to have made a commitment to risk management. Third, when risks are assessed, their impacts must be incorporated into project plans. Some projects carry out risk assessments but don't do anything with the risk information they obtain. That is roughly comparable to sending your calls to voice mail and never checking your messages.

Developing the ability to perform risk management is partly straightforward, partly subtle. The straightforward part is that the project team carries out the activities described in this section. The subtle part is that some organizations inadvertently discourage the flow of risk-oriented information to upper management and other people who need it. The plan described in this section helps to ameliorate that problem.

This book's approach employs some practices that are intended primarily to manage risk. Other practices described in this book are not specifically risk-management practices but have been built into the approach because of their risk-management benefits. Practices recommended specifically for risk management include the following:

- Planning for risk management in the Software Development Plan (which is what this section has been describing)

- Identification of a risk officer

- Use of a Top 10 Risks List

- Creation of a risk-management plan for each risk

- Creation of an anonymous risk-reporting channel

These practices are described in the next few sections.

RISK OFFICER

The project should identify a risk officer, who is a member of the project (preferably someone other than the project manager) responsible for spotting emerging risks. The risk officer must be part Chicken Little ("the sky is falling") and part Eeyore ("it'll never work"). The risk officer's function is to play devil's advocate during planning meetings and when reviewing planning materials. Continually looking for potential problems, the risk officer tries to pick apart the risk-management plans for each risk. He or she should have management's respect; otherwise, the risk officer simply becomes the project's "designated pessimist."

Often a senior developer or tester makes a good risk officer. Because the project manager's job is to steer the project to success, the project manager can have difficulty adopting the devil's advocate focus that the job of risk officer requires. The risk officer's role in the project is parallel to the independent tester's role in testing code; it is too hard for developers to try to make and then break the code at the same time. The two jobs require different orientations, and the jobs of project manager and risk officer do too.

Identification of a risk officer doesn't eliminate the need for other project personnel to try to reduce project risk. The information flow patterns and reward criteria within the organization should encourage risk identification by all project personnel.

TOP 10 RISKS LIST

The key risk-management tool is the Top 10 Risks List, which is a list of the top risks the project faces at any given time. The simple act of maintaining a list of current risks helps to keep risk management at the forefront of the project manager's mind.

The project team should create a preliminary risks list before beginning requirements work and then keep the list current through the end of the project. It isn't important that the list contain exactly 10 risks. It can contain 5 risks or 15. What is important is that it is maintained regularly. The project manager, risk officer, and the project manager's boss should review the Top 10 Risks List every two weeks or so. This review should be on their biweekly schedule so that the activity isn't abandoned. The act of updating the risks list, prioritizing the risks, and updating the "Risk Resolution Progress" column forces them to think about risks regularly and to be alert to changes in the risks' importance.

In support of the survival skill of projectwide visibility, the list should be made available to all project personnel. People who are not in the management chain should be encouraged to sound an alarm if they identify significant problems at their level. This list can be simple, such as the one shown in Table 7-2 (on pages 98–99).

TABLE 7-2 **SAMPLE TOP 10 RISKS LIST**

This Week	Last Week	Weeks on List	Risk	Risk Resolution Progress
1	1	5	Creeping requirements	User Interface Prototype used to gather high quality requirements.
				User Manual/Requirements Specification has been placed under explicit change control.
				Staged delivery approach will be employed to provide some ability to change features if needed.
2	5	5	Requirements or developer gold-plating	Vision statement specifies what is not included in software. Design emphasis placed on minimalism.
				Reviews have checklist item for "extra design or implementation."
3	2	4	Released software has low quality	User Interface Prototype developed to assure users will accept software.
				Disciplined development process is used.
				Technical reviews are used on all requirements, designs, and code.
				Test planning assures all functionality will be covered by system testing.
				System tests are performed by independent testers.
4	7	5	Unachievable schedule	Project avoids making schedule commitment prior to completing requirements specification.
				Upstream reviews are used to detect and correct problems when it is least expensive to do so.
				Schedule is reestimated several times over the course of the project.
				Active project tracking assures that any schedule slips will be detected early.

(continued)

TABLE 7-2				**SAMPLE TOP 10 RISKS LIST** *continued*
This Week	**Last Week**	**Weeks on List**	**Risk**	**Risk Resolution Progress**
				Staged delivery allows for delivery of partial functionality even if whole project takes longer than expected.
5	4	2	Unstable tools delay schedule	Only one or two new tools are used on this project; remainder have been used on previous projects.
6	-	1	High turnover	Project vision encourages developer buy-in.
				Active, detailed project planning creates clear expectations.
				Periodic reestimation supports revised plans to account for changes in scope without massive overtime.
				Productivity environment supports high developer productivity, high motivation, and high retention.
7	3	5	Friction between developers and customers	User Interface Prototype aligns developers and customers on same detailed vision.
				Staged deliveries provide customers with evidence of steady progress.
8	6	5	Unproductive office space	Will move development to off-site environment with private offices after completing User Interface Prototype.
				Still need budget approval for conducting project off-site.

Tool Support for Risk Tracking

An alternative to creating the Top10 Risks List is to enter the risks into the defect tracking system (separately from the project's defects). Defect tracking systems will typically allow risks to be marked open or closed. They can be assigned to specific project team members for resolution. They can be prioritized. You can print out lists of them arranged by priority, by the amount of time they've been open, and by person responsible for resolving them. You can track the steps taken to resolve them, who took the step, and so on. A defect tracking system can take some of the tedium out of maintaining the risks list.

DETAILED RISK-MANAGEMENT PLANS

Each risk on the Top 10 Risks List should be supported by a detailed risk-management plan. The risk-management plans do not need to be elaborate; they can take up only a page or two each. The risk-management plan should answer the questions shown in Table 7-3.

TABLE 7-3   **RISK-MANAGEMENT PLAN**

Why?
Why is a risk-management plan needed for this specific risk? Describe the risk's probability of occurrence, consequences, and severity.

How?
How will the risk be resolved in general? Describe the general approach to resolving the risk. List or describe the options that were considered.

What?
What specific steps will be taken to resolve the risk? List the specific steps and deliverables that will be generated in addressing the risk.

Include a description of the conditions under which the risk will be upgraded—for example, if the risk cannot be resolved by a specific date.

Who?
Who will be responsible for completing each step? List the specific person responsible for completing each step.

When?
When will each step be completed? List the completion date for each step.

How much?
How much budget is allocated to the resolution of the risk? List the cost of each step that will be taken to resolve the risk.

Anonymous Risk-Reporting Channel

Reporting good news projectwide and up the management chain seldom poses problems, but reporting bad news often does. The project team should establish an anonymous communication channel that project members can use to report status and risk information up the management chain. This "channel" can be as simple as a suggestion box in the project break room. If developers are turning their code over to testing later than scheduled, a concerned tester can report that. If testers are releasing builds to documentation that have not been well tested, a concerned tech writer can report that. If project management is exaggerating the project's progress in reports to upper management, a concerned developer can report that.

If you're in top management, and some technical person predicts 10 to 20 percent of the way through the project that the project isn't going to work, you want to know that prediction after 10 to 20 percent of the project has elapsed, not after 150 percent has elapsed and that technical person says, "I tried to tell you but couldn't get past my first-level manager."

The project home page in Figure 7-1 on page 93 suggests a way that an anonymous reporting channel could be incorporated into a project's home page. When this approach is used, a list of anonymously reported risks is available to all project personnel at all times.

Personnel Strategies

To support the peopleware survival skill described in Chapter 4, I recommend the use of "people-aware management accountability." The idea behind this long phrase is that managers should be held accountable for whether the organization's human resources emerge from a project strengthened or diminished. Do five developers quit the company at the end of the project? That's a tangible loss to the company and should be held against the manager just as losing $250,000 would be. Does the whole development team emerge from the project with improved skills and incredible morale? That's a tangible benefit to the organization and should be credited to the manager's account.

PERSONNEL DEVELOPMENT

The project plan should contain explicit provisions for emerging from the project with enhanced human resources. Here are some characteristics of plans based on people-aware management accountability:

- Managers are evaluated based on how well they retain project personnel.

- All members of the project have access to professional growth opportunities during the project.

- Developers believe in the vision of the project and emerge from the project feeling better about the company, not worse.

STAFF BUILDUP

The most efficient way to staff a medium-sized project is to staff the project with senior personnel during the requirements stage, then add staff during the architecture and design stages. During requirements analysis and architecture, the best work is done by small teams of about two to five people. A project shouldn't begin to staff up until it passes its Planning Checkpoint Review 10–20 percent of the way through the project. Larger groups tend to dilute the conceptual integrity of the software and increase the project's burn rate without adding productivity. The later stages of detailed design and construction can support much larger teams and remain productive. But new people must be added by the early stages of construction, or the late personnel addition can actually decrease the overall project productivity.

For small projects (those with about seven or fewer developers), using a flat staffing model in which all team members are present on the project the entire time is effective.

New Developers: Available vs. Good

When a project is staffed, avoid the trap of hiring developers just because they are available; hold out for those who are qualified. On a 12-month project, waiting a month or two to hire a qualified programmer is usually a better strategy than hiring a less capable programmer who's available earlier.

One of the most widely replicated results of software engineering research is that at least a 10 to 1 difference in productivity exists between the most effective developers and the least effective ones. This does not mean that the most effective developers are 10 times as productive as some nominal productivity level. It means that they are 5 times as productive as the nominal level while the least productive programmers actually drag the project backward. Avoid hiring those least productive developers even if they are readily available.

———◆———

It's better to wait for a productive programmer to become available than it is to wait for the first available programmer to become productive.

———◆———

Team Dynamics

One of the more interesting research results of the past 10 years was published in 1993 by a researcher named B. Lakhanpal. Lakhanpal's study examined 31 teams to determine which had more impact on productivity: individual developer's capabilities or team cohesion. The study found that team cohesion had a greater impact on productivity than did the team members' individual capabilities. Individual capabilities scored a close second.

The implication of this study is startling. Teams are usually assembled based solely on the technical competencies of individual team members. But this study implies that when a team is assembled, at least as much attention should be paid to how well the team members will work together. Once an especially cohesive team has formed, the careful manager will think twice about automatically disbanding it at the end of a project and will look for ways to keep it together.

Once the project is under way, don't tolerate troublesome developers. In another study of 75 projects, Larson and LaFasto found that the single biggest complaint that team members had about their team leaders was the failure to address problem personnel. The team members all knew who the problem team members were but gave their leaders low marks for dealing with them. Paradoxically, team leaders tended to score themselves high in this category.

If you suspect a team contains a difficult person, work as quickly as possible with the project manager, upper management, human resources department, or whoever else needs to be involved to move the person off the project or out of the company. The negative productivity effect of reduced team cohesion, which affects every team member, will outweigh whatever positive contribution the difficult team member is thought to be making. Moreover, in the cases I've seen, after the difficult team member leaves the project, the quality of that person's work is inevitably discovered to be on the same level as that person's personal interactions—poor. There is no advantage to delaying the removal of a difficult team member.

Key Staff-Buildup Questions

Here are the key questions about project staffing that the preliminary project planning should address:

◆ Does the project manager have software experience with one or more projects of a similar size?

◆ Does the project's senior technical staff have knowledge of the kind of software being built and experience on similar successful projects?

◆ Most teams are comprised of average personnel. Do expectations about the team's productivity match the team members' abilities?

◆ Will the individuals work well together?

TEAM ORGANIZATION

Different organizations use a variety of approaches to team organization, and some organizations are definitely more effective than others. The most effective software organizations treat their senior software developers and managers as equals. They treat their software managers the same way that professional athletic teams treat their managers: they are critically important to the success of the team, but no more than the star players are.

Project Team Organization

A project team, no matter what size, needs to differentiate among the various roles played by team members. On small projects, several roles may be performed by one person.

◆ *Project manager.* The project manager is responsible for orchestrating the detailed technical work of the project, including development, quality assurance, and user documentation. The project manager is responsible for developing the project's software development plan and is usually the development team's link to upper management.

◆ *Product manager*. The product manager is responsible for integrating project work at the business level. On commercial software products, this work includes marketing, product packaging, end-user documentation, end-user support, and the software itself. On in-house projects, this work includes working with groups that will use the system to define the software, setting up training and user support, and planning for cut over to the new system.

◆ *Architect*. The architect is responsible for the conceptual integrity of the software at the design and implementation level.

◆ *User-interface designer*. The user-interface designer is responsible for the conceptual integrity of the software at the level visible to the user. On in-house projects, this role can be played by someone from end-user support, user documentation, development, or product management. On commercial products, it should be performed by a user-interface specialist.

◆ *End-user liaison*. The end-user liaison is responsible for interacting with end users throughout the project—walking them through the prototype, demonstrating new releases, eliciting user feedback, and so on. This role can be performed by a developer, product manager, or someone from end-user support.

◆ *Developers*. Developers are responsible for the detailed design and implementation of the software. Developers are responsible for making the software work.

◆ *QA/Testers*. The quality assurance personnel plan and manage test activities, create detailed test plans, and perform tests. They are responsible for finding all the ways to make the software break. If the project is large enough, these people may have their own QA lead or manager.

◆ *Tool smith*. The tool smith is responsible for developing build scripts, maintaining the source-code control system, developing specialized utilities needed by the project, and so on.

◆ *Build coordinator*. The build coordinator is responsible for maintaining and running the daily build (discussed in Chapter 14) and for notifying developers when their source code breaks the build.

◆ *Risk officer*. The risk officer is assigned to watch for emerging risks, as described earlier in this chapter.

◆ *End-user documentation specialists*. These specialists are responsible for generating help files, printed documentation, and other instructional materials that end users will use.

You might think this list identifies a lot of different roles, but most projects perform all these roles either formally or informally. I have found that it is useful to explicitly identify each role for planning purposes even if the day-to-day responsibilities of the role are carried out informally. On large projects that assign one or more whole people to each role, the work involved in each role is self-evident. Indeed, larger projects will have additional, more specialized roles than those listed here. On smaller projects in which each person performs several roles, it can be easy to underestimate the full scope of a person's responsibilities during project planning—for example, overlooking the fact that a key developer is also responsible for most of the interactions with end users. Explicitly defining roles helps to ensure that each person's full responsibilities are considered in the project's schedule and other project plans.

Most of the roles can be intermingled in whatever way makes sense for the specific project, but the roles of development and quality assurance should not be intermingled. The quality assurance roles require a devil's advocate mind-set that is difficult or impossible for developers to adopt.

Tiger Teams

A well-run project will identify short-term, high priority tasks throughout its lifetime. The project team might need to determine whether a code-library update eliminates problems the team has had with previous versions of the library. It might need an in-depth assessment of a new release of a competitor's product. Or it might need to extend the project's User Interface Prototype in response to user feedback generated by a midproject release.

In such cases, the project manager can appoint a "tiger team" to tackle the problem. A tiger team is a small team (usually one or two people) who perform a single task quickly—usually in two weeks or less, often in just a few days. Once team members have accomplished their assignment, they disband and return to their regular assignments. Preliminary planning should include time for as-yet-to-be-determined tiger team assignments.

Be aware that each developer responds to tiger team assignments differently. Some developers view a tiger team assignment as a recognition of their contributions and will be offended if they are never assigned to one. Some staff members appreciate the chance to work on something different for a while and to take a break from the project. Others do not like the distraction of being diverted from their primary work.

Rotating assignments among staff members is an effective approach to creating tiger teams: if the project leaders always assign their most effective developers, they can delay the main work of the project while driving those developers crazy with distractions. Sometimes a project manager can find individuals who thrive on short-term assignments; in such cases, the project manager can juggle those individuals' assignments to provide them with more chances to participate on tiger teams.

TIME ACCOUNTING

The early part of a project is also a good time to begin detailed time accounting, that is, keeping track of how project personnel spend their time. Time accounting is a critical component of project visibility and control on the current project and lays the foundation for more accurate estimates and planning on future projects.

Time-accounting data enables you to compare estimated time to actual time with the goal of improving future estimates. You can use the breakdown of time spent on activities from one project to help plan future projects. You can review the amount of time spent on rework and get an idea about whether enough time is being spent on correcting defects close to their sources.

If an organization doesn't have its own time-accounting categories, your project can use the time-accounting categories shown in Table 7-4 on pages 108–109.

Time accounting should begin as early in the project as possible, otherwise valuable historical information that can be used to plan future projects will be lost. The time-accounting categories need to be about as detailed as those shown in Table 7-4. Any less detailed and the time-accounting data won't contain enough detail to provide guidance in planning future projects. Projects that use time accounting typically employ any one of several networked time-accounting programs that allow team members to enter their own time data from their desks. (Pointers to various time-accounting programs can be found on the *Survival Guide* Web site.)

TABLE 7-4   **SAMPLE TIME-ACCOUNTING CATEGORIES***

Time-Accounting Category	Activity
Management	Plan
	Track progress/status
	Report progress/status
	Manage project team activities
	Manage customer/end-user relations
	Manage change
Administration	Downtime
	Lab setup
Process development	Create development process
	Review development process
	Rework development process
	Educate customer or team members about development process
Requirements development	Create User Manual/Requirements Specification
	Review User Manual/Requirements Specification
	Rework User Manual/Requirements Specification
	Report defects detected during requirements development
User-interface prototyping	Create User Interface Prototype
	Review User Interface Prototype
	Rework User Interface Prototype
	Report defects detected during prototyping
Architecture	Create architecture
	Review architecture
	Rework architecture
	Report defects detected during architecture

---

* This time-accounting table is available in electronic form from the *Survival Guide* Web site.   *(continued)*

TABLE 7-4   **SAMPLE TIME-ACCOUNTING CATEGORIES** *continued*

Time-Accounting Category	Activity
Detailed design	Create detailed design
	Review detailed design
	Rework detailed design
	Report defects detected during detailed design
Implementation	Create implementation
	Review implementation
	Rework implementation
	Report defects detected during implementation
Component acquisition	Investigate/acquire components
	Manage component acquisition
	Test/review acquired components
	Maintain acquired components
	Report defects in acquired components
Integration	Automate build
	Maintain build
	Test build
	Distribute build
System testing	Plan system testing
	Create manual for system testing
	Create automated system test
	Run manual system test
	Run automated system test
	Report defects detected during system test
Software release	Prepare and support alpha, beta, or staged release
	Prepare and support final release
Metrics	Collect measurement data
	Analyze measurement data

The Software Development Plan

The plans created at this time are less detailed than the plans that will be in place by the end of the project, but these plans should still be committed to writing. Ineffective software projects are often characterized by a revisiting of the same issues again and again. Because these issues form the planning foundation for the project, it is important that they be recorded. A document called the Software Development Plan should describe the planning considerations outlined in this chapter, including decision-making authority, project scope, publicizing of plans and progress, risk management, personnel strategies, and time accounting.[1] Once drafted, the plan should be reviewed and signed off by the project manager, quality assurance group, and the development team. It should then be placed under change control just as all other important work products are.

Once plans have been created for one project, they can more easily be modified and adapted for use on future projects. The plan for the very first project takes more effort than future plans will.

---

1. A detailed, annotated outline of a Software Development Plan is available from the *Survival Guide* Web site.

Survival Check

👍 The project has a clear vision.

💣 The vision doesn't provide guidance in deciding what to leave out of the software.

👍 The project team has identified an executive sponsor or committee with final authority over projectwide decisions.

👍 The project plans and progress compared to the plans are readily available to all project team members and upper management.

👍 The project has a risk officer.

💣 The risk officer is the project manager.

👍 The project has a Top 10 Risks List.

💣 The Top 10 Risks List is not kept up to date.

👍 The project team develops risk-management plans for each risk on the Top 10 Risks List.

👍 The project leaders hire well-qualified people (waiting for qualified people, if necessary), rather than just hiring whoever is available first.

👍 Time accounting is begun before requirements development begins.

👍 All of the above considerations are formalized in a Software Development Plan.

💣 The Software Development Plan isn't placed under change control.

💣 The Software Development Plan isn't actually followed by the development team.

8
Requirements Development

During requirements development, the software concept becomes tangible through the creation of several versions of the User Interface Prototype and the User Manual/Requirements Specification. This approach facilitates gathering the best possible set of requirements, lays a foundation for excellent architecture work, streamlines the project by eliminating the time-consuming detailed requirements document, and keeps user documentation off the critical path.

S oftware requirements development is the part of the project during which the needs of the customer are gathered and translated into a specification of what the system must do. Requirements development consists of three related activities:

♦ Gathering candidate requirements, which is accomplished by interviewing the potential users about the system they want, reviewing competitive products, building interactive prototypes, and so on.

♦ Specifying requirements, which is accomplished by committing the gathered requirements to tangible media, such as a written requirements document, project storyboards, an interactive User Interface Prototype, or some other medium.

♦ Analyzing requirements, which is accomplished by looking for commonalities and differences among requirements and breaking them down into their essential characteristics. (This is a preliminary design activity and is not discussed further in this chapter.)

I depart somewhat from common terminology in referring to these activities as requirements *development*. These activities are often referred to as "specification," "analysis," or "gathering." I use the word *development* to emphasize that requirements work is usually not as simple as writing down what key users want the software to do. Requirements are not "out there" in the users' minds waiting to be gathered in the same way that iron ore is in the ground waiting to be mined. Users' minds are fertile sources of requirements, but the project team must plant the seeds and cultivate them before the requirements can be harvested.

———◆———

The most difficult part of requirements gathering is not the act of recording what the users want; it is the exploratory, developmental activity of helping users figure out what they want.

———◆———

Requirements gathering and specification is an open-ended activity. You can consider the project team to be finished with requirements only when it has achieved a clear, stable understanding of what the users want the software to do. Abbreviating requirements activities is a costly mistake. For each requirement that is incorrectly specified, you will pay 50 to 200 times as much to correct the mistake downstream—during coding—as you would pay to correct the mistake at requirements time.

OVERVIEW OF THE REQUIREMENTS DEVELOPMENT PROCESS

Here are the general steps I recommend to develop requirements:

1. Identify a set of key end users who collectively have the credibility to define the software that the team is building.

2. Interview the end users to create a set of preliminary requirements.

3. Build a simple, interactive User Interface Prototype.

4. Show the simple User Interface Prototype to the key end users and solicit their feedback. Continue revising the simple prototype, keeping it simple, showing it to the end users, and revising it again until the end users are excited about the software concept.

5. Develop a style guide that codifies the prototype's look and feel, review it, and put it under change control.

6. Fully extend the prototype until it demonstrates every functional area of the software. Make the prototype broad enough to cover the whole system, but keep it as shallow as possible. It should demonstrate the functional area, not actually implement it.

7. Treat the fully extended prototype as the baseline specification. Put it under change control. Then require the developed software to match the prototype exactly, except for changes approved through the change control process.

8. Write the detailed end-user documentation based on the prototype. This detailed end-user documentation will become the detailed software specification, and it should also be put under change control.

9. Create a separate, non–user-interface requirements document for algorithms, interactions with other hardware and software, and so on. Put that document under change control.

This set of steps is weighted heavily toward development of interactive software. If the software you are developing is an embedded system that doesn't have a user interface (such as an automobile cruise control), much of the discussion in this chapter won't apply to your project.

The following sections describe the nuances of the steps in the requirements process.

IDENTIFY A SET OF KEY END USERS

The first step in gathering requirements is to identify a set of users who will provide guidance in defining software requirements. These users must be selected in such a way that if they say that a feature is important, you can believe that it truly is important. Likewise, if they say that a feature can be left out, you should be confident that you truly can leave it out. Be sure to include both power users and average users.

If the project is in-house software, the project leaders can recruit a handful of actual users and make the users' involvement with the project part of their job descriptions. If the project is shrink-wrap software, the project leaders can still recruit a handful of actual users. In order to use their time efficiently, they'll need to make sure that interactions with the users are more planned and structured.

Soliciting user input is a critical success factor. What if you can't find any end users and the project grinds to a halt? That might be a blessing in disguise. The project is better off burning only calendar time while you try to find end users than burning both calendar time and money while you build software that users will ultimately reject.

INTERVIEW THE END USERS

An initial set of user interviews should be conducted to elicit a preliminary set of requirements. The preliminary set of requirements is used as the basis for creating the initial, simple User Interface Prototype.

If we've learned one thing in the last 20 years about software developers' abilities to design software that users like, it's that software developers by themselves aren't very good at designing software that users like. But software developers can be very good at helping users discover what they like, because users by themselves aren't very good at designing software they like either.

BUILD A SIMPLE USER INTERFACE PROTOTYPE

Keep the prototype as simple as possible. The point of this activity is to present many alternatives to the user before you commit much effort to any particular approach. The project team should develop just enough to give the user the look and feel of the software they're going for, and nothing more. If you want to prototype a report format, for example, don't even bother to have the User Interface Prototype print the report. The developers should only mock up the report in a word processor and tell the users, "Here's what will come out when you hit the print button."

If the project is being developed in an environment that doesn't have good prototyping tools, consider prototyping on a Windows-based machine and mimicking the look and feel of the target platform. If the real development environment is an IBM mainframe, for example, use Microsoft Visual Basic to mock up screens with green characters and black backgrounds.

Prototyping activity should be performed by a small team of about one to three senior developers. These developers should be skilled at demonstrating a software's look and feel with the *least* amount of work possible. If developers are taking more than a couple of hours to develop the prototype for any single part of the software, they are doing too much work; they are developing the prototype with too much functional depth. Keep it as shallow as possible.

Developing the prototype in this way helps users visualize the software they are specifying, which minimizes the problem of users not knowing what they want until they see it and then changing their minds later in the project. This kind of prototyping reduces the risk of creeping requirements, which is traditionally one of the most serious risks a software project faces.

———◆———

Be sure the users understand that the prototype is "just a prototype." One risk of creating a User Interface Prototype is accidentally raising unrealistic expectations about future progress on the project.

———◆———

USE PAPER STORYBOARDS IF POSSIBLE

One low-tech approach to User Interface Prototypes is paper storyboards. In this approach, developers or end users start the prototyping process by drawing pictures of the screens, dialogs, toolbars, and other elements they would like the software to have. Developers and end users meet in groups and draw sample screens on flip charts. They work out the details of the software by simply redrawing the prototype on flip charts until they reach agreement about the software's appearance and functionality.

This approach offers several advantages. Users can do some of the work themselves; they don't have to know how to use prototyping software. Storyboard prototypes can be generated and modified rapidly. They are inexpensive.

Paper storyboards also eliminate some of the most common risks associated with prototyping. On the developer side, they eliminate the risk of needlessly overextending the prototype and of spending too much time fiddling with the prototyping tools. On the user side, storyboards eliminate the problem of users thinking that a realistic-looking prototype is almost the real software.

The one disadvantage of paper storyboards is that some developers and end users simply cannot visualize the software from a paper mock-up. This is a significant disadvantage since the strongest reason to create a prototype is to help the users visualize the software that will be built. If you find that paper storyboards aren't helping the project stakeholders visualize the software, don't hesitate to revert to electronic prototypes.

REVISE THE PROTOTYPE UNTIL THE END
USERS ARE EXCITED ABOUT THE SOFTWARE

The first version of a prototype will rarely satisfy the users' expectations. Developers should show it to the users with the expectation that the users will have comments that will cause the developers to revise the prototype. They should explain to the users that the prototype is a work in progress and that they want the users' criticism. If the users are confused or think the software will be hard to use, that isn't the users' fault; that's a problem that should be corrected during prototyping, before work on the actual software begins. Prototype development will take more time if the development team is working in a new area (one in which it has less than two years of experience) rather than in a familiar area.

Refining the simple prototype until users are excited about it supports creation of software that will ultimately be highly satisfactory to end users rather than software that merely "satisfies requirements." It might seem as though developers are spending an inordinate amount of time working on something that will be thrown away, but this upstream activity is a good investment in preventing costly downstream problems.

While revising the prototype, remind users that it is "just a prototype." In one organization I worked with, when developers reminded the users that they were seeing "just a prototype," the users started chanting, almost in unison, "and it's just smoke and mirrors, and it will still take a long time to develop. We know, we know, we've heard that before." The users were good-natured about the reminder; the developers had done a good job of educating them.

DEVELOP A STYLE GUIDE

Once the users have agreed to the general look and feel of the prototype, the developers should create a User Interface Style Guide that sets standards for the application's look and feel.[1] This style guide should be only a few pages long including screen shots but be complete enough to guide remaining work on the prototype. It should include the size and placement of standard buttons such as OK, Cancel, and Help; allowable fonts; the style of error messages; mnemonics for common operations; adherence to common design standards; and other common elements of the user interface. After it is developed, the User Interface Style Guide should be reviewed and put under change control.

Addressing design style issues early in the project promotes a consistent user interface. It also prevents developers from continually tweaking the user interface and prevents users from requesting arbitrary, late changes to the software when it is finally delivered.

---

1. For an example of a prototype style guide, see the *Survival Guide* Web site.

FULLY EXTEND THE PROTOTYPE

Driving prototype development across the full breadth of the system enables developers to visualize the software to a degree that promotes better architecture and design work. The project's vision statement enables developers to align their work in a general way; the detailed User Interface Prototype provides the detailed vision that enables them to align their work in thousands of smaller ways.

Be sure that the prototype truly addresses all of the software's functionality. Here is a partial list of the functionality that should be represented:

- All dialog boxes, including standard dialogs such as File Open, File Save, Printing, and so on

- All graphical input screens

- All graphical and textual outputs

- Interactions with the operating system, such as importing and exporting data to the clipboard

- Interactions with all third-party products, such as importing and exporting data to other programs, providing components to be embedded in other programs, and so on

At the time the prototype is baselined, the development team will probably be unclear about whether implementing some of the specific functionality demonstrated in the prototype is technically feasible. This question about feasibility is a natural aspect of prototyping, since it is easy to prototype functionality that couldn't be implemented in a million years. (For example, you could easily prototype a system that draws a photographically realistic picture based on a textual description typed in by the user, but actually implementing that is well beyond the current or foreseeable state of the art.)

A list of functionality that is at risk should be documented, explained to the end users, signed off, and put under change control. This list can be included as a section in the requirements specification. It is a rare project that will not have any functionality in this category, so you should expect to have a list of "to be determined" areas on your project.

REMEMBER THAT IT'S A THROWAWAY PROTOTYPE

Although the prototype is driven across the full breadth of the software, the emphasis should continue to be on demonstrating functionality with the least possible amount of work. Remember that the prototype is a dead end. It is a useful dead end, but a dead end nonetheless.

A good prototype is slapped together quickly with programming duct tape and baling wire. It is like a Hollywood stage set in which the front of a piece of wood is painted to look like a house but the back of the piece of wood has no house connected to it.

———◆———

*You shouldn't use a User Interface Prototype
as the basis for real software any more than
you should use a Hollywood stage set as the
basis for a real house.*

———◆———

When a prototype is developed in this way, do not under any circumstances use it as the code base for releasable software. It has intentionally been developed to be disposable; trying to use its code in the releasable software is tantamount to trying to build a real house on the foundation of the Hollywood stage set house.

Consider developing the prototype in a programming environment that makes it clear that the prototype code will not find its way into the final software. If the project team is planning to implement the software in C++ or Java, for example, develop the prototype in Microsoft Visual Basic so that it would be impractical to use it as the basis for the real software.

TREAT THE FULLY EXTENDED
PROTOTYPE AS THE BASELINE SPECIFICATION

By this time, the prototype can begin to serve as the reference point to which the whole development effort will be aligned. For it to serve that function, it must be stable and the team must commit to developing software that exactly matches the prototype. The project's decision makers must sign off on it and put it under change control. The organization will base its estimates, plans, staffing, architecture, designs, and development work on it. It is both appropriate and necessary that the decision makers commit to the prototype and that changes to it be systematically controlled.

Systematically controlling changes does not mean "freezing" the requirements. Instead, the project is making a commitment to handle further changes to the software in strategic ways that support the project's objectives. The most common alternative approach is to handle changes indiscriminately, with no strategic plan, in ways that ultimately impair the project's ability to achieve its objectives.

Once the prototype has been baselined, it provides several valuable benefits. In addition to the requirements stability benefits already described, a full User Interface Prototype enables end-user documentation and test plans to be developed in parallel with architecture, design, and implementation work. Otherwise, these activities often end up on the critical path because they cannot be started until implementation is well under way.

WRITE THE DETAILED END-USER DOCUMENTATION BASED ON THE PROTOTYPE

Sometime prior to placing the prototype under change control, work can begin on a detailed user documentation (called the User Manual/Requirements Specification). This is the documentation that will eventually be delivered to the software's end users. Typically, this documentation is developed at the end of the project, but in this book's approach, it is developed near the beginning.

Some people might object that creating full-up end-user documentation and keeping it up to date takes more time than creating a purely technical requirements spec. That's true as far as the requirements spec alone is concerned, but creating the User Manual/Requirements Specification is often cheaper than developing end-user documentation and a full technical spec.

Developing end-user documentation first eliminates the necessity of producing a stand-alone technical specification. The document that is produced is more understandable to end users than is the typical technical spec, which improves the quality of end-user feedback about the software. The early development of the end-user documentation fleshes out the details of the software demonstrated by the User Interface Prototype, filling in gaps and flushing out inconsistencies.

This approach involves end-user advocates in the project early on— technical writers tend to be good at representing the end user's point of view, often with more sophistication than the end users themselves are capable of.

This kind of spec is more likely to be kept up to date. Many requirements specifications become "write-only" documents—they are written at requirements time to satisfy the project plan's edict to create a requirements specification, but they aren't kept up to date with requirements changes and often aren't even used after they are written. They are too monolithic and too boring. In contrast, when the development team knows that the spec will ultimately be released to end users, it has a greater incentive to keep the spec up to date.

This approach also solves the perennial problem of whether the requirements spec should cover the "what" or the "how." If the technical writers think the end users need to know something, what they need to know should be in the User Manual/Requirements Specification. Anything that's not covered in this specification is left to the developers' discretion.

Many products contain complex documentation sets that include a user manual, tutorial, reference, and online help. The only item that needs to be created during the prototype development stage is a document that describes the end-to-end functionality of the software. If this document is envisioned as part of the online help, developing the online help *first* will provide the most useful reference for the development team.

CREATE A SEPARATE, NON–USER-INTERFACE REQUIREMENTS DOCUMENT

The approach described in this chapter works best for user intensive, small- to medium-sized projects. Most projects will have some functionality that cannot be specified in enough detail in a User Interface Prototype or user manual to provide guidance for design and implementation. Specifications of detailed algorithms, interactions with other hardware and software, performance requirements, memory usage, and other less visible requirements can be recorded in a separate requirements document (or as an appendix to the User Manual/Requirements Specification). After its initial development, that document (or appendix) will need to be reviewed, baselined, and placed under change control.

Survival Check

👍 The project team identifies a set of key end users who can be trusted to shape the software.

👍 The developers create several versions of a basic prototype until they find one that the users are excited about.

💣 Prototyping stops while users are still only lukewarm about the prototype.

👍 The developers extend the User Interface Prototype to elicit detailed requirements from users.

💣 The prototype is not kept broad and shallow, and time is wasted providing deep functionality that will be rewritten for the final software.

👍 The project team develops a User Manual/Requirements Specification to use as the detailed requirements specification.

👍 The fully developed prototype is baselined and placed under change control.

💣 The project team attempts to use the prototype code in the real software.

👍 A separate, non–user-interface requirements document is created, reviewed, and placed under change control.

9
Quality Assurance

Software quality assurance used to be thought of exclusively as testing, but on effective projects it now encompasses testing, technical reviewing, and project planning—all oriented toward early, economical detection and correction of defects.

P eople mean many different things when they talk about "quality." Quality can refer to the absence of system crashes. It can refer to the correspondence between the software and the users' expectations, or to the intangible fit and finish of a program. It can refer to the conformance to specified requirements, or to the specification of correct requirements in the first place. A good general definition of quality is "the degree to which the software satisfies both stated and implied requirements." This chapter explains how to assure that kind of quality.

Why Quality Matters

Even if your software doesn't have to be ultra reliable, keeping defects under control matters because it affects development speed, development cost, and other project characteristics. Chapter 3, "Survival Concepts," described the upstream/downstream effect: defects cost 50 to 200 times as much to correct if they are detected and corrected downstream instead of upstream. That should be enough reason to focus on quality, but other bottom-line impacts exist as well.

People sometimes think they can take quality shortcuts on their current project and then correct them on the next project. On the smallest projects (those with durations of one to two months or less), a project team can sometimes cheat the hangman. On longer projects, quality shortcuts turn out to be self-defeating. It isn't possible to defer all the bad effects arising from quality shortcuts to the *next* project; many of those effects will affect the *current* project.

Software quality has a bottom-line impact on the costs of doing business. Low quality software increases the burden on end-user support. Leading-edge companies such as Microsoft have recognized this by charging end-user support costs back to the business unit that produced the software responsible for the support call.

Developing low quality software and then building upon that shaky foundation also increases maintenance costs. You might think that your program will be around for only 3 to 5 years, but the average program actually survives long enough for 10 generations of maintenance programmers to support it. Since 50 to 80 percent of the lifetime cost of a program tends to be incurred after the program's initial release, it makes good financial sense to have version 1 lay the groundwork for success rather than failure.

Finally, only you can decide what effect releasing low quality software will have on your business. My strong impression is that customers do not remember that high-quality software was delivered late or that low quality software was delivered on time as much as they remember whether they like using the software.

———◆———

The problem with quick and dirty,
as some people have said, is that dirty remains
long after quick has been forgotten.

———◆———

THE QUALITY ASSURANCE PLAN

One of the themes of this book is that organizations intending to survive a software project must *commit* to surviving the project. Software project survival requires a commitment to quality assurance, which involves at least these elements:

- Software quality assurance activities must be planned.

- The plan for the software quality assurance activities must be committed to writing.

- Software quality assurance activities must begin during software requirements activities or earlier.

- A separate group for performing software quality assurance must exist. Depending on the size of the project, that "group" might consist of one person. It might even consist of two developers from two different one-person projects swapping quality assurance work on each other's projects.

- Members of that group must be trained in how to perform software quality assurance activities. It is not sufficient to point to the least senior programmer and say, "You there. You are now the quality assurance department."

- Adequate funding must be provided for performing software quality assurance activities.

ELEMENTS OF THE QUALITY ASSURANCE PLAN

An effective Quality Assurance Plan will call for several quality assurance activities: defect tracking, unit testing, source-code tracing, technical reviews, integration testing, and system testing.

Defect tracking runs throughout these quality assurance activities. The project team keeps records of each defect found, its source, when it was detected, when it was resolved, how it was resolved (fixed or not), and so on. Defect tracking is a critical element of project tracking and control. Good defect information helps determine how far the project is from release, what its quality is, and where the greatest potential for improved efficiency in the development process lies.

Unit testing is informal testing of source code by the developer who wrote it. The word "unit" can refer to a subroutine, a module, a class, or an even larger programming entity. Unit testing is usually performed informally but should be required for each unit before that unit is integrated with the master sources or turned over for independent review or testing.

Source-code tracing is stepping through source code line by line in an interactive debugger. This work is performed by the developer who wrote the code. Many developers have found this to be an invaluable means of detecting coding defects, and my own experience bears this out. Anecdotal evidence suggests that projects that require developers to step through their code in a debugger before integrating it experience far fewer integration problems than projects that don't use source-code tracing.

Technical reviews are reviews by developers of work their peers have completed. These reviews are used to assure quality of the User Interface Prototype, requirements specification, architecture, designs, and all other technical work products. New source code and source code changes should also be reviewed. Technical reviews are generally conducted by the development team. The quality assurance staff's role in the reviews is to ensure that they are being carried out and to track defects detected during the reviews.

Integration testing is exercising newly developed code in combination with other code that has already been integrated. This kind of testing is carried out informally by the developer who developed the new code.

System testing is the execution of software for the purpose of finding defects. System testing is performed by an independent test organization or quality assurance group.

Taken in combination, this set of quality assurance activities might seem to result in a lot of overhead, but in actuality exactly the opposite is true. The point of a multi-layered quality assurance approach is to detect as many defects as possible as early as possible to keep the costs of corrections down.

DEFECT TRACKING

Defect tracking is the activity of recording and tracking defects from the time they are detected until the time they are resolved. Defects are tracked both at the individual level—that is, defect by defect—and at the statistical level, in terms of number of open defects, percentage of defects resolved, average time required to correct a defect, and so on.

Beginning defect tracking early in the project increases the awareness of the importance of eliminating defects early and, over the course of a project, provides the most accurate information about the number of defects detected in the software.

Defect tracking should begin early in the project, preferably by the time requirements have been baselined, after a work product is placed under change control. When a programmer discovers a design defect at implementation time, that defect should be tracked because the design has been baselined. If the same coder discovers a coding error in new code that has not yet been baselined, that defect shouldn't be tracked. But if the coder discovers the same defect after the code has been reviewed and baselined, that defect should be tracked.

Defect reports should be placed under change control. Making all defects public provides valuable data about software quality and allows the project team to estimate the number of defects remaining in the software. Counts of defects removed should be used to track progress during testing activities.

This defect tracking might sound like a lot of drudge work, but it doesn't have to be. Many specialized tools are available to make this work almost painless.[1] Table 9-1 on the following page lists the information that should be tracked for each defect.

---

1. For a current list of such tools, see the *Survival Guide* Web site.

TABLE 9-1   **INFORMATION TRACKED IN A DEFECT REPORT**

Defect ID (a number or other unique identifier)

Defect description

Steps taken to produce the defect

Platform information (CPU type, memory, disk space, video card, and so on)

Defect's current status (open or closed)

Person who detected the defect

Date the defect was detected

Severity (based on a numeric scale such as 1-4, or a verbal scale such as cosmetic, serious, critical, and so on)

Phase in which the defect was created (requirements, architecture, design, construction, defective test case, and so on)

Phase in which the defect was detected (requirements, architecture, design, construction, and so on)

Date the defect was corrected

Person who corrected the defect

Effort (in staff hours) required to correct the defect

Work product or products corrected (requirements statement, design diagram, code module, User Manual/Requirements Specification, test case, and so on)

Resolution (pending engineering fix, pending engineering review, pending quality assurance verification, corrected, determined not to be a defect, unable to reproduce, and so on)

Other notes

Collecting this defect information enables the project team to create graphs and reports that are useful for tracking and assessing project status as well as for developing a base of information that is useful on future projects. (Chapter 16, "Software Release," describes in more detail about how to use this information.)

TECHNICAL REVIEWS

Because of their ability to detect and correct defects in upstream work products, technical reviews are at least as important in controlling cost and schedule as testing is. The generic term "technical review" refers to any of several review techniques including walkthroughs, inspections, and code reading.

In addition to their quality assurance benefit, reviews serve as a time during which junior and senior developers can "cross-pollinate." Senior developers can fix problems in junior developers' code, and junior developers can learn more about their craft by reading senior developers' code. Reviews also provide a chance for junior developers to present new methodologies and challenge old assumptions.

GENERAL REVIEW PATTERN

Reviews follow a general pattern:

1. *Notification and distribution.* The author of the work product notifies the reviewers that the work product (for example, the project plans, requirements, User Interface Prototype, design, code, or test case) is ready to be reviewed. In formal settings, the author will give material to a moderator, who will decide who should review the work product and who should attend the review meeting. Material is distributed for review.

2. *Preparation.* Reviewers review the work product, preferably aided by a checklist of errors that have been most common in the past. The review meeting should be held only after reviewers have completed their reviews of the work product.

3. *Review meeting.* The author, moderator (if there is one), and reviewers meet to examine the work product.

4. *Review report.* After the meeting, the author or moderator should log the statistics for the review meeting—the amount of material reviewed, number and kind of defects detected, amount of time spent in the review meeting, and whether the work product passed or failed the review.

5. *Follow-up.* The author or some other person makes any required changes, the changes are reviewed, and the work product is declared to have formally passed the review.

KEYS TO SUCCESS IN USING REVIEWS

For best results, pay attention to the following key points:

Begin reviews early in the project   Technical materials created during requirements, architecture, and design should all be reviewed. Quality assurance materials such as the Quality Assurance Plan and test cases should be reviewed by both quality assurance and technical staffs. Reviews should continue through implementation. All detailed designs and source code should be reviewed. Management work products, including the project schedule and Software Development Plan, should also be reviewed.

Keep technical reviews focused on defect detection   During a technical review, the focus should be on *detecting problems*. Spending meeting time creating and evaluating solutions typically wastes the time of at least some of the people in the review meeting and is best handled as a separate activity.

Keep technical reviews technical   If reviews are not focused, they can degenerate into technical chest thumping contests. The presence of any sort of authority figure at a technical review changes the focus to impressing the authority figure, and for that reason neither management nor customers should be allowed to attend. Reviews for the benefit of management or customers might well be appropriate, but they are not technical reviews in the sense described here and should be conducted separately.

Keep track of what material has been reviewed   Tracking review progress of designs and code becomes another useful measure of the project's status. By tracking the number of modules reviewed per week, you can know how many modules have yet to be reviewed. If the project reviews many more modules than average in a week in order to meet a deadline, the reviews might have been superficial; testing may expose more defects than average in those modules.

Record the defects detected during reviews   The work product that comes out of a review is a review report. The review report should list the defects detected and provide a schedule for corrections and for verifying the corrections.

Verify that work identified during the review is performed   One common weakness of technical reviews is that the project doesn't follow up on the defects identified during the review. For this reason, the defects detected during a technical review should be entered into the defect tracking system just as the defects detected during system testing are. That allows the defects to be tracked until they are closed, just as other defects are.

Make review results public to the project team   Although the review itself should contain only technical personnel, review results should be made public (within the project team, not beyond it) so that they can be used by other members of the project. This would allow, for example, developers to juggle their schedules and delay writing code that interfaced with an error-filled module—a module that had so many errors it would have to be rewritten.

Allow time in the schedule for reviews and for correcting problems identified during reviews   Reviews cannot be effective if the project's leaders expect them to be completed in addition to the developers' "normal" work. On a successful project, reviews are an integral part of developers' normal work and should be scheduled just as the rest of their work is.

If reviews are effective, they will detect problems in the plans, designs, test cases, or source code under review. The schedule should include time to correct the problems identified during the review.

System Testing

Reviews are a critical means of assuring software quality upstream. System testing is the critical means of assuring it downstream. Here are some of the keys to successful software system testing.

Conduct system testing by using independent testers   To be effective, software needs to be tested by personnel other than the developers who created it. Developers can find a certain number of defects in their own code, but finding the maximum number of defects requires a shift in mind-set from making the software work to making it break, and precious few developers are capable of wearing both those hats on the same project.

Begin test planning as soon as requirements are known   Effective system testing depends on effective planning. Test cases need to be designed, reviewed, and implemented just as source code does. If you don't want testing to become the critical path activity that holds up release of your software, be sure test planning begins as early as possible—as soon as requirements are known.

Begin system testing during Stage 1   In a staged delivery approach, executable software will become available midway through the first stage, and system testing should begin then.

Ensure full requirements coverage with a requirements traceability matrix   Software system testing should be planned so that it covers 100 percent of the software's functionality. This is typically assured through a process called "requirements traceability," in which a large matrix is created with test cases in the rows and requirements in the columns. A "1" in a row and column indicates that that row's test helps to verify that column's requirement. A row without a "1" indicates that the row's test case doesn't verify any requirement, is not needed, and can be eliminated. A column without a "1" indicates that no test case has been created to verify that column's requirement. Every column and every row should have at least one "1." Creation of the requirements traceability matrix is monotonous work, but it is the best way to ensure that the full range of the software is being tested.

Provide adequate resources for system testing   The resources required to adequately test computer software vary depending on the kind of software being developed. For high-quality commercial software, a ratio of one tester per developer is a good rule of thumb. This is the ratio used at Microsoft and other top software companies. This number of testers is required because most of the test suite needs to be automated so that quality assurance can test the software end-to-end as often as the software changes, sometimes as often as every day. Some mission-critical business systems will also require this much testing.

For life-critical software, a greater number of testers is required. The flight control software for the space shuttle used 10 testers per developer.

At the other end of the scale, in-house business systems that do not have to be ultra reliable require a smaller testing commitment, perhaps as few as one tester per three or four developers. The test cases do not have to be fully automated and the software does not have to be quite as reliable, so the testing requirements are less demanding.

Break the testing addiction cycle   Testing by itself doesn't improve software quality any more than stepping onto a scale by itself can make a person lose weight.

————◆————

Testing is a means of discovering the quality level of a software system, not a means of assuring software quality.

————◆————

When testing is combined with defect correction, the test-and-fix combination constitutes a means of assuring software quality, but not a very effective one. A more effective approach is to combine upstream quality assurance activities, such as user interface prototyping and technical reviews, with downstream testing; this approach is both more economical and more effective.

The lack of upstream quality assurance activities locks many organizations into a damaging "test addiction" cycle. Their software has poor quality because too little work has been performed upstream, which leaves huge numbers of defects to be detected downstream. Because of the huge numbers of defects, many testers are needed on the low quality project, which makes it hard to allocate the quality assurance resources needed for effective upstream work on the next project. As more resources are devoted to downstream testing on one project and less to upstream prevention on the next project, the addiction worsens; the next project will experience even more downstream problems and need even more downstream testing.

The only way to break the testing addiction cycle is to bite the bullet and allocate the upstream resources needed for quality assurance on a project. Once the beneficial results of that approach are seen on one project, it will become easier to obtain upstream resources for the next project.

BETA TESTING

Under this book's recommended approach, general quality assurance is addressed through the *internal* practices of technical reviews and system testing by an independent testing organization. But companies release software to external beta testers for a variety of reasons, which are summarized in Table 9-2. Some of the reasons listed are technical; most are nontechnical. The important thing to realize is that all of the technical reasons to use beta testing are better served through means other than beta testing, with the possible exception of compatibility testing.

TABLE 9-2   REASONS TO USE OUTSIDE BETA TESTING*

1. *Expert consulting.* Some organizations show the software to expert users to see what the experts will think about it and to change it to be more appealing to the experts.

2. *Magazine reviews.* Some organizations show software to magazine reviewers prior to releasing it to the general public in order to garner favor with them.

3. *Customer relationship building.* Some organizations release beta software to their key customers to let those customers know that they receive preferential treatment.

4. *Testimonials and spin control.* Organizations sometimes release software to the general public in order to get complimentary statements about the software, which can then be used in marketing materials. Other organizations gather customer comments to identify popular and unpopular aspects of the software and then emphasize the most popular aspects in their marketing materials.

5. *Polishing the user-interface design based on customer usage patterns.* Some organizations put their nearly complete software into customers' hands so that they can observe how customers use it, with the goal of fine-tuning the software to overcome commonly experienced difficulties.

6. *Compatibility testing.* Some organizations release beta software to customers so that they can determine how well it runs with a wider variety of hardware and software environments than they have available in-house.

7. *General quality assurance.* Some organizations put their software into as many users' hands as possible, under the assumption that the more users who use the software, the more defects they will find prior to release.

* Sources: Adapted from *Testing Computer Software, 2d Ed.* (Kaner, Falk, Nguyen 1993) and *Software Project Dynamics* (McCarthy 1995).

Expert consulting during beta testing is a case of too little, too late. If you want expert consulting, get it at requirements time in response to the

User Interface Prototype. Polishing the user interface design is another case of too little, too late, and should also be handled at requirements time rather than at beta test time.

General quality assurance was once the primary reason for beta testing, but software companies have found that external beta testing is no bargain. When companies first sent out beta software, most of the people who received the software didn't report any defects, and they often didn't return any comments at all. So organizations started to restrict to whom they would give beta software. But then they found themselves overwhelmed by requests from beta users to change the software, and they still weren't receiving defect reports. After experiences like this, organizations realized that beta testing produces lots and lots of low quality feedback and doesn't serve a useful quality assurance purpose, though it might serve useful marketing purposes.

If you want feedback from real end users, pay representative users to come to the project's facilities and use the software under supervision instead of conducting a widespread beta test program. Videotape the users' entire session with the software so that the development team can reproduce any problems the users encounter. Supervised user testing will produce more focused feedback than beta testing. For this reason, the leaders in the commercial software industry have largely moved away from using beta testing for quality assurance purposes.

—◆—

An effective beta test program requires
a great deal of coordination and typically
diverts resources that could provide more
quality assurance benefit if focused
inside the organization.

—◆—

If your software will ultimately be distributed to users numbering in the thousands, however, you'll probably want to create some external releases before you create the final release. These external releases are not for general quality assurance but for specific compatibility testing. Not even the richest organizations can afford to purchase and exhaustively test the incredible variety of hardware and software combinations found on modern desktops. Once the software has been thoroughly system tested, the only practical way to perform compatibility testing is to release it to a set of forgiving external users.

Work Products Covered by the Quality Assurance Plan

The Quality Assurance Plan should indicate the work products that will be reviewed or tested. Table 9-3 describes the quality assurance practices that should be applied to each of the work products in this book.

TABLE 9-3   RECOMMENDED QUALITY ASSURANCE PRACTICES AND RESPONSIBILITIES FOR THIS BOOK'S WORK PRODUCTS*

Work Product	QA	Development	Documentation	Management	Customer/ Marketing	End User
Change Control Plan	●	●	●	●	●	○
Change Proposals	●	●	●	●	●	○
Vision Statement	●	●	●	●	●	○
Top 10 Risks List	●	●	●	●	○	
Software Development Plan, including estimates	●	●	●	●	○	
User Interface Prototype	● □	●	●	○	●	●
User Interface Style Guide	●	●	●	○	○	●
User Manual/ Requirements Specification	● ■	●	●	○	●	○
Quality Assurance Plan	●	○		○	○	
Software Architecture	○	●		○	○	
Software Integration Procedure	○	●	○	○		
Staged Delivery Plan	●	●	●	●	●	○
Individual Stage Plans, including miniature milestone schedules	●	●	●	○	○	

*   Definitely reviewed (●) or tested (■). Possibly reviewed (○) or tested (□).

(continued)

TABLE 9-3   RECOMMENDED QUALITY ASSURANCE PRACTICES AND RESPONSIBILITIES FOR THIS BOOK'S WORK PRODUCTS *continued*

Work Product	QA	Development	Documentation	Management	Customer/ Marketing	End User
Coding Standard		●		○		
Software test cases	●	○		○		
Executable software	■	■	■	■	■	■
Source code (new)	○ ■	● □		○ □		
Source code (changes)	○ ■	● ■		○ □		
Media, including graphics, sound, video, and so on	○ ■	● ■	○	○	●	○ □
Software build instructions (make files)		●				
Detailed Design Documents	○	●		○		
Software Construction Plan for each stage	○	●	○	○		
Install program	○ ■	● ■	○	○	○	■
Deployment Document (Cutover Handbook)	○ ■	● ■	●	●	●	● ■
Release Checklist	●	●	●	●	○	
Release Approval	●	●	●	●	●	
Software Project Log	○	●	○	○		
Software Project History Document	○	●	○	○	○	

As you can see, every work product placed under change control is reviewed, and some are also tested. Some work products such as the user manual are "tested" in the sense that someone actually punches every keystroke described in the manual and verifies that it works as documented.

Specific responsibilities can vary quite a bit from one project to another, especially depending on the skills and interests of the specific documenters, managers, customers, marketers, and end users involved with the project.

SUPPORTING ACTIVITIES

In addition to their explicit quality assurance activities, the quality assurance group will participate in the preparation and review of the project's Software Development Plan, standards, and procedures. The QA group will review the software development activities to verify that reviews, unit tests, and source-code tracing are performed. It will periodically report the results of its activities to developers and management, and will periodically review its activities with senior management.

SOFTWARE RELEASE CRITERIA

In many of the organizations I review for the consulting side of my business, the sole determination of when to release the software lies with the software development organization. This is too much like putting the fox in charge of the chicken coop. Developers and development managers are eager to meet their schedule targets and to believe that their software has excellent quality. A set of checks and balances is needed to counteract that natural tendency, and the quality assurance group provides that.

For this reason, the Quality Assurance Plan must specify in *measurable* detail what the release criteria for the software are. The release criteria can be something like "zero reproducible software crashes," or "mean time to defect of 8 hours," or "95 percent of all reported defects corrected," or "no uncorrected 'Sev 1,' or 'Sev 2' errors." The release criteria must be measurable so that the quality assurance group can report whether the software is ready to release without having to make a politically unpopular judgment call.

Survival Check

 Project has a written, approved Quality Assurance Plan.

 Project isn't following the written plan.

 Quality assurance is initiated in parallel with requirements work.

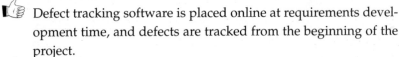 Defect tracking software is placed online at requirements development time, and defects are tracked from the beginning of the project.

 Developers review all designs and code before the designs and code are considered "done."

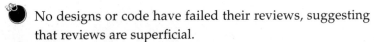 No designs or code have failed their reviews, suggesting that reviews are superficial.

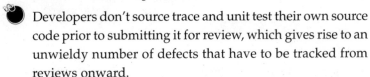 Developers don't source trace and unit test their own source code prior to submitting it for review, which gives rise to an unwieldy number of defects that have to be tracked from reviews onward.

 The Quality Assurance Plan calls for an independent quality assurance group.

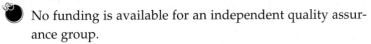 No funding is available for an independent quality assurance group.

 The Quality Assurance Plan contains measurable criteria that are used to determine whether the software is ready to be released.

10 Architecture

Software architecture provides the technical structure for a project. Good architecture makes the rest of the project easy. Bad architecture makes the rest of the project almost impossible. A good Software Architecture document describes overall program organization, ways in which the architecture supports likely changes, components that can be reused from other systems or purchased commercially, and design approaches to standard functional areas. It also minimizes potential downstream costs by enumerating how the architecture addresses each system requirement.

In building construction, the architecture phase is a time during which a general plan for a building is mapped out through the use of scale models and blueprints before the building is actually constructed. Scale models and blueprints provide a means of exploring alternatives more cheaply than using steel, concrete, and other building materials.

In software development, the architecture phase is a time during which the software is mapped out through the use of design diagrams and prototypes. As in building construction, the architecture phase provides a means of exploring alternatives at relatively low cost. Typically the architecture, which is also known as "system architecture," "design," "high-level design," and "top-level design," is described in a document referred to as the Software Architecture document.

During the architecture phase, the architecture team partitions the system into major subsystems, specifies all the interactions among subsystems, and documents the software's top-level technical plans. The team also addresses the major design issues that run throughout the system, such as the approaches to error handling, memory management, and string storage. Architecture paves the way for detailed design work by defining the structure that the detailed designs will use.

On small projects, architecture and design might be rolled into one activity, but on most projects, architecture should be treated as a separate activity. Fred Brooks, author of *The Mythical Man-Month*, reports that, "Having a system architect is the most important single step toward conceptual integrity…. After teaching a software engineering laboratory more than 20 times, I came to insist that student teams as small as four people choose a manager and a separate architect. Defining distinct roles in such small teams may be a little extreme, but I have observed it to work well and to contribute to design success."

The discussion in this chapter assumes that the software architecture is developed by a small team of architects. Regardless of exactly how the roles are conceived, the issues described in this chapter should be considered carefully and addressed before proceeding with detailed design and construction.

EASING INTO ARCHITECTURE

Architectural work should begin when requirements development is about 80 percent complete. Resolving 100 percent of the requirements before beginning architectural work usually isn't possible without delaying the project.

By the time 80 percent of the requirements are known, the project is on firm enough footing to support creation of the software architecture. Eighty percent is a rule of thumb, and the project leaders will need to use their own judgment on any specific project to evaluate whether requirements have been sufficiently developed for architecture to begin.

Before the architecture team begins architectural work in earnest, however, the project team, upper management, and the customer should hold the Planning Checkpoint Review described in Chapter 4. Plunging into full-fledged architectural development is pointless if the project isn't going to be funded.

CHARACTERISTICS OF A GOOD ARCHITECTURE

When the architecture team does plunge into architectural development, they'll face a set of core design issues, which the project's architecture should address.

SYSTEM OVERVIEW

A system's architecture needs to describe the system in broad terms. Without such an overview, developers will have a hard time building a coherent picture from a thousand details or even a dozen individual modules or classes. The architecture should also contain a high-level discussion of the major design alternatives that were considered, the reasons that the selected approaches were chosen, and the reasons the other alternatives were not selected.

CONCEPTUAL INTEGRITY

The objectives for the architecture should be stated clearly. A design for a system with a primary goal of modifiability will be different from a design for a system with a goal of uncompromised performance, even if these systems have the same function.

A good architecture should fit the problem, whatever it is. After days or weeks of wrestling with the architectural design, the architect should create an architecture that addresses the problem so well that when other people see the architecture they say, "That seems obvious; how else could you do it?" Harlan Mills referred to this quality as "deep simplicity." An architecture that is more complicated is worse, not better.

Beware of kitchen-sink architectures—architectures that try to address every conceivable aspect of every conceivable problem. It should be clear from the architecture developed that the architecture team has taken advantage of opportunities to simplify its approach. As one measure of simplicity, the best architecture documents are short, diagram-intensive, and average less than 100 pages.

The central thesis of the most popular software engineering book ever, *The Mythical Man-Month*, is that the essential problem of large systems is maintaining their conceptual integrity. When you look at the architecture, you should be pleased at how natural and easy the solution is. It shouldn't look like the problem and the architecture are stuck together with duct tape.

SUBSYSTEMS AND ORGANIZATION

The architecture should define the major subsystems in a program. Subsystems are major clusters of functionality, such as output formatting, data storage, analysis, user input, and so on. Most systems should contain five to nine subsystems—with many more, the system will be too hard to understand at the architectural level. Figure 10-1 shows the appropriate level of detail for subsystem design in an application program.

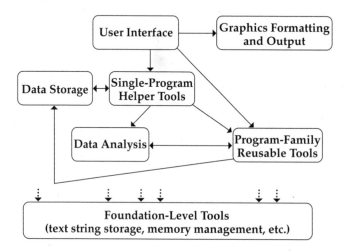

FIGURE 10-1   *Example of subsystem architecture diagram. Most architectures have five to nine top-level subsystems. Good architectures have relatively few interactions among their subsystems.*

In addition to a diagram like the one in Figure 10-1, the architecture should describe the responsibilities of each subsystem and provide a preliminary list of the modules or classes that will be contained within each subsystem. The final list will be developed during detailed design and construction.

The architecture should describe what communications are allowed among the different subsystems. In Figure 10-1, only a few inter-subsystem communications are allowed. Figure 10-2 illustrates what happens when there are no rules guiding how subsystems communicate with one another: subsystems interact in every possible combination, which undermines the goal of minimizing complexity. A good architecture holds communications among subsystems to a minimum.

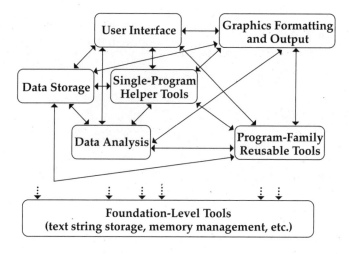

FIGURE 10-2   *Example of architecture without rules limiting communication among subsystems. Without communication limitations, architectures become uncontrollably complex.*

Restrictions on communication among subsystems typically cannot be enforced automatically by standard software development tools. Conformance to architectural guidelines should therefore be a line item on the checklists used for detailed design and code reviews. Be aware, however, that developers who haven't worked on projects with well-developed architectures sometimes resist the restrictions the architecture places on their coding.

—◆—

*Once you realize that the goal of architecture is to
reduce complexity, it becomes clear that the
architect must focus as much on what to leave out
of the software as on what to put in.*

—◆—

NOTATION

For large projects, the project should adopt a standard notation such as the
Booch/Rumbaugh Unified Modeling Language (UML) notation. For smaller
projects, just be sure that everyone understands what the diagrams mean
and that the diagrams are readily available in a public location.

Later in the project, at detailed design time, the development team may
use the same notation it used for the architecture or one that's appropriate
for more detailed design work. If it uses UML for the architecture, it might
want to continue using it. The development team might also begin using
pseudocode to express the designs of individual routines. Regardless of what
it chooses, the development team should agree upon the specific notation at
architecture time so that it will be used projectwide.

CHANGE SCENARIOS AND CHANGE STRATEGY

One key feature of a successful architecture is the identification of program
areas that are most likely to change. Some of the most damaging influences
on a project are late, unexpected changes to the software—changes that occur after the design is complete and while implementation is under way.
Projects that deal poorly with such changes can run into trouble even if they
are under control up to the point at which the changes are introduced. So the
architecture should list the most likely changes to the program and outline
how each change will be addressed. One common source of changes is shaky
requirements, so the architecture should include a list of the requirements
that are the least stable.

Another common source of problems is changes in supporting technology—for example, the developers find that the company that provided
the class library they have been using has gone out of business. Be sure the
project isn't bound to any single-source technology (compiler vendor, hard-

ware platform, and so on). Where that's not possible, be sure the architecture contains firewalls so that the developers can recover if that single-source technology becomes unreliable.

In considering change scenarios, strive to elaborate about 80 percent of possible scenarios, and then stop. The architecture team cannot possibly anticipate every possible change, and by the time it has elaborated 80 percent of the scenarios, it will have reached a point of diminishing returns.

REUSE ANALYSIS AND BUY VS. BUILD DECISIONS

One key component of the architecture is the identification of which components will be purchased commercially, which will be reused from internal sources, and which will be created from scratch.

The project's approach to reuse will affect the rest of the software's design, so it should be defined at architecture time. If the architecture team decides to base an application on a commercial application framework, for example, the rest of the software will need to be designed around that framework. Another reason that reuse should be considered at architecture time is that the approach to reuse has a dramatic cost and schedule implications. One of the most powerful ways to shorten a software schedule and reduce costs is to buy components or reuse existing software instead of building new software.

The architecture team should not limit its reuse considerations to source code; it should also consider how to reuse data, detailed designs, test cases, plans, documentation, and even architectural components—all of which can sometimes be used again.

APPROACHES TO STANDARD FUNCTIONAL AREAS

In addition to system organizational issues, the architecture should focus on the handful of design decisions that have the most sweeping implications for detailed implementation. Here are some of the most common functional areas the architecture should address:

◆   *External software interfaces.* Is the software expected to communicate with other software? What is the function call protocol? Which data structures are passed across the program interfaces, and what do they look like?

◆ *User interface.* How is the user interface isolated from the rest of the system so that changes to the interface won't affect other software components?

◆ *Database organization.* What is the organization and content of the database?

◆ *Data storage.* How is nondatabase data stored? What file formats are used? What are the major data structures?

◆ *Key algorithms.* What are the software's key algorithms? Have they been well defined, or is part of the software project's mission to define new algorithms?

◆ *Memory management.* What is the strategy for allocating memory to different program elements?

◆ *String storage.* How are text strings such as error messages stored and retrieved?

◆ *Concurrency/threads.* Is the software multi-threaded? If so, how are concurrency, re-entrancy, and related issues handled?

◆ *Security.* Is the software required to operate in a secure environment? If so, how is the software's design affected?

◆ *Localization.* Is the software expected to work in countries that use a language other than the language for which the software was originally targeted? How are different text strings, different character sets, and possibly different page orientations (right to left instead of left to right) handled?

◆ *Networking.* How does the software support multiuser operations on a network?

◆ *Portability.* How does the software run in more than one environment (for example, in both UNIX and Microsoft Windows NT)?

◆ *Programming language.* Does the architecture allow the software to be implemented in any programming language, or does it require the software to be implemented in a specific language?

◆ *Error handling.* Does the architecture contain a coherent error-handling strategy?

REQUIREMENTS TRACEABILITY

The architecture team should create a "traceability matrix" like the one described for test case coverage in Chapter 9, "Quality Assurance."

Creation of this requirements traceability matrix is typically a tedious job. It can also be frustrating because just when the architecture team thinks it has completed the architecture, it finds a handful of requirements that aren't satisfied by any of the subsystems. Frustrating or not, when the team finds an unsatisfied requirement, congratulations are in order! The time the team spends finding and correcting that architecture error is 50 to 200 times less than the time it would have spent detecting and correcting that same error during construction or system testing.

---◆---

If you're going to get bad news on a software project, it's best to get it early because of the upstream/downstream effect on project costs.

---◆---

During requirements development, the project team should have created a list of functional areas that were at risk because of uncertainty about whether those functions could be implemented. By the time the architecture is complete, most of the items on that list should be resolved—the architecture team will have outlined ways to implement them, or it will have decided that the items can't be implemented and it will eliminate them from further consideration.

SUPPORT FOR THE STAGED DELIVERY PLAN

One final characteristic of the architecture is of critical importance for projects that use this book's approach. The architecture must support the Staged Delivery Plan. The Software Architecture document should explain how the architecture accommodates the development and delivery of the planned functionality in the stages contained in the Staged Delivery Plan. Specifically, it should not depend on subsystems that have to be implemented all at once and that cannot be broken into stages. It should identify the dependencies among different parts of the system and map out a plan for developing the different parts in an order that supports the Staged Delivery Plan.

Architecture is typically a time when you run into some resistance to staged delivery. Staged delivery will require the architecture team to make some "nonoptimal" architectural decisions, such as creating temporary scaffolding code that might not be needed if some other approach were used, or requiring extra code to minimize dependencies among subsystems. The important question to keep in mind is, "Nonoptimal for *what?*" An architecture that doesn't deliver critical functionality until the end of the project is not optimal. Neither is an architecture that depends on an implementation strategy that contains so much risk that the project is likely to be canceled. The architecture cannot be designed solely with static, end-system goals in mind. It must also be designed with dynamic, development process goals in mind.

HOW TO TELL WHEN ARCHITECTURE IS COMPLETE

Knowing when the architecture team is finished with the architecture is a genuine challenge. On the one hand, you shouldn't declare the architecture to be done until the architecture team is willing to bet the project on it—until the architecture team is willing to consider their architecture "frozen" and proceed with the project. You don't actually freeze the architecture, but the architecture team should be that confident in it.

On the other hand, the architecture will never be perfect, and at some point the development team just has to plunge into the rest of the project. The team won't have perfect knowledge of all the project design issues until the project is well into coding, so you shouldn't expect the architecture to be perfect.

———◆———

Follow the advice given to the team that designed the Algol programming language: "The best" is the enemy of "the good."

———◆———

If you try for the best, you often end up with nothing. Strive for minimalism, simplicity, and coverage of all requirements, and don't worry too much about finding the single best solution.

Be sure that activities and deliverables are well defined and closely monitored. The architecture team can easily spin its wheels during the architecture phase, causing the phase to be nonproductive.

THE SOFTWARE ARCHITECTURE DOCUMENT

Once the architecture is complete, it should be described in the Software Architecture document, submitted to the change control board, circulated for review, revised as needed, and baselined. The Software Architecture document then becomes the standard that controls future design and development work. Be sure to enforce the architecture through the technical review process. There is no point in creating an architecture unless it is implemented throughout the rest of the project.

As further work is done, the architecture will inevitably need to be revised. When that happens, the architecture should be updated through the usual change control process. Following that process ensures that the architecture isn't changed capriciously, and it helps highlight the true costs of architecture defects compared to downstream detailed design and construction defects.

Survival Check

 The architecture team creates a Software Architecture document.

 The Software Architecture document has not been placed under change control.

 The Software Architecture document has not been updated to reflect changes arising during design and construction, and it no longer accurately describes the software.

Developers don't observe the project's architecture.

 The architecture emphasizes simplicity over cleverness.

 The architecture supports the Staged Delivery Plan.

 The architecture addresses all the project's requirements, and requirements coverage is documented with a completed requirements traceability matrix.

11

Final Preparations

The final preparations period builds on and extends the preliminary planning that was performed before the requirements development and architecture phases. At final preparations time, the project team is ready to create its first estimates, develop a plan to deliver its most important functionality first, and refine its other plans.

P reparing for survival on a well-run software project is an ongoing activity. After the project team has baselined the requirements and begun architecture, it can create more detailed plans than were possible in the early stages of the project. I refer to this point in the project as "final preparations time." During this time, some of the earlier plans will need to be revised to reflect changes in the software concept that occurred during requirements development. Other plans will need to be filled in using information that became available after requirements were baselined.

This chapter describes the preparation work that should be done after the project requirements have been baselined and architecture work is under way. This work includes the following tasks, each of which is discussed in this chapter:

- Creating project estimates
- Writing a Staged Delivery Plan
- Performing ongoing planning activities

In addition to the tasks I just listed, the project team will need to engage in another kind of planning before it can begin detailed implementation— the specific planning for the next staged delivery cycle, planning which is conducted at the beginning of each stage. That is discussed in the next chapter.

PROJECT ESTIMATES

As soon as requirements have been baselined, the project team can create meaningful estimates for effort, cost, and schedule. Keep these rules of thumb about software estimation in mind:

1. It is possible to estimate software projects accurately.
2. Accurate estimates take time.
3. Accurate estimates require a quantitative approach, preferably one supported by a software estimation tool.
4. The most accurate estimates are based on data from projects completed by the organization doing the current project.
5. Estimates require refinement as the project progresses.

ESTIMATION PROCEDURE GUIDELINES

Effective organizations follow a systematic estimation procedure.[1] To be effective, the estimation procedure should include the following characteristics.

The estimation procedure should be written   A written procedure can prevent overly ambitious project managers, upper managers, marketers, and customers from browbeating the development team into adopting an unachievable effort or schedule estimate. Part of the value of an estimation procedure is that project estimates *must* be created according to the procedure.

———◆———

Once all project stakeholders agree to the estimation procedure, you can engage in rational negotiations about the inputs to the estimate (feature set and resources) rather than irrational arguments about just the outputs (budget and schedule).

———◆———

Estimates should be created by an expert estimator or by the most expert development, quality assurance, and documentation staff available. Good estimation requires expertise in software project estimation. If you can find an expert estimator, make use of that person's services. If no expert is available, the estimate should be created by the person with the most experience doing similar work. Regardless of whether an expert is available, be sure the project's estimates include input from the people most familiar with the kind of work being estimated.

Estimates should include time for all normal activities   Table 11-1 on the next page lists some of the obvious and not-so-obvious activities that should be included in a project estimate.

---

1. You can download a sample estimation procedure from the *Survival Guide* Web site.

Table 11-1 Activities That Should Be Included in a Project Estimate

Obvious Activities

Architecture

Detailed design

General planning

Planning for each staged release

Coding

Testing

Creating user documentation

Creating installation program

Creating program to convert data from old system to new one

Less Obvious Activities

Interacting with customers or end users

Demonstrating the software or prototype of the software to upper management, customers, and end users

Reviewing plans, estimates, architecture, detailed designs, stage plans, code, test cases, and so on

Fixing problems detected during reviews and testing

Maintaining the revision control system

Maintaining the scripts required to run the daily build

Assessing impacts of proposed changes

Answering questions from quality assurance

Answering questions from documentation

Supporting old projects

Involvement in tiger teams

Receiving technical training

Training personnel who will support the software

Holidays

Vacations

Weekends

Sick days

Some projects adopt short-term attitudes and consciously plan to exclude many of the activities listed in Table 11-1. That approach can work for a small project, but on any project that lasts longer than a few weeks (which is any project long enough to need the plan described in this book), these activities creep back into the project in one form or another. And because these activities aren't accommodated in the project plan, the ever-widening gap between the plan (what the team is supposed to be doing) and reality (what is really happening on the project) creates a dangerous risk to the project: the project team stops taking the project's goals seriously. At that point, the project team loses its ability to create meaningful plans, track progress, and control the project.

The project plan should not assume the team will work overtime   If the project plan assumes that the team will work overtime, the project won't have any reserves to draw from if it gets behind. Beginning a project that has overtime built in from the start is like beginning a hike in the mountains in the winter without carrying extra food and warm clothes. Everything will work out okay if you're lucky, but what sensible person wants to depend on being that lucky?

———◆———

*To minimize the risk of schedule overruns, add
more resources at the beginning of the project
instead of creating plans that depend on overtime.*

———◆———

Estimates should be created using estimation software   A commercial software estimation tool can serve as an objective authority in estimating a software project. The best tools provide lists of tasks, project roles, and detailed schedules tailored to specific kinds and sizes of projects.[2]

Using estimation software can prevent a common destructive dynamic that leads to confrontational negotiations about cost and schedule. Suppose one of the project's stakeholders—we'll say marketing—rejects an initial estimate because it is too high. Trying to be cooperative, marketing then proposes a few minor cuts and in turn expects dramatic reductions in the project's cost and schedule.

In cases like this, estimation software can serve as an impartial third party. Changes in assumptions about the project can be entered into the software, and the software can arbitrate the effect on the project's cost and schedule.

---

2. You can download my company's estimation software, Construx Estimate, at no charge from the *Survival Guide* Web site. The site also contains pointers to other commercial estimation software.

Estimates should be based on data from completed projects   The best source of estimation data you have is time and effort data drawn from completed projects within the same organization. Good software estimation programs allow estimators to calibrate their estimates using data from their own organization's projects.

Estimators sometimes make the mistake of using *planning* data from previous projects; don't use planning data from other projects unless *actual* data is unavailable.

Watch for estimates that developers don't accept   On projects in trouble, I often find that developers thought the project estimates were unrealistic from the start. Developers did not have a chance to review the estimates before the estimates were presented to upper management or to the customer. Lack of buy-in from developers is at best a warning sign that the project's goals are unachievable. At worst, it indicates an adversarial relationship between developers and management, which means the project probably has serious motivation and morale problems in addition to the problems it has from overcoming planning errors caused by inaccurate estimates.

The project team should plan to reestimate at several specific times during the project   As I mentioned in Chapter 3, "Survival Concepts," estimating a project precisely in its early stages isn't even theoretically possible. As Chapter 7, "Preliminary Planning," described, the most effective software organizations plan to revise their estimates several times over the course of a project. The use of a Planning Checkpoint Review with a two-phase funding approach builds reestimation into the project plans at the top management level.

Although, in this book, the section on estimation follows the chapter on architectural design, estimates should be made at the *end* of these specific phases:

- Preliminary requirements development (after the User Interface Prototype is developed)

- Detailed requirements development (after the User Manual/ Requirements Specification is complete)

- Architectural design

Estimates should be placed under change control   After the project team has completed the estimates at each phase, the estimates should be reviewed, signed off, and baselined just as other critical work products are. One of the advantages of putting estimates under change control is that estimates must be reviewed and approved by all concerned parties—a rogue customer, manager, or marketer cannot unilaterally foist a well-meaning but unfounded estimate on the project. Similarly, a development team can't slip a new schedule into the project in the middle of the night—schedule changes will be visible to all the people affected by the changes.

MILESTONE TARGETS

The project team should use the newly created estimates to set completion date targets for the project's major milestones, bearing in mind that these milestone targets will be revised and become more accurate as the project progresses. The Software Development Plan should include dates for the following major milestones:

◆   Architecture complete

◆   Stage 1 complete

◆   Stage 2 complete

◆   Stage 3 complete

◆   Software release (assuming only three stages)

In addition to major milestone targets, as the project progresses, the Software Development Plan should be updated to include detailed milestone targets for whatever phase comes next. (At this point in the project— that is, final preparations—the next phase is Stage 1. Details about Stage 1 are described in the next chapter.)

NONTECHNICAL CONSIDERATIONS IN ESTIMATION

Software project estimation is a double-barreled problem. The first part of the problem is that estimation itself is technically difficult. The guidelines described in the preceding section outline what is needed to overcome those difficulties.

The second part of the problem is that estimation is made even more difficult by pressures from marketers, managers, customers, and other project stakeholders who want the estimates to turn out more to their liking.

It is not uncommon for an organization to use the most advanced estimation software available, base its estimates on the past performance of the people who will build the new software, and then have an uninformed executive cut the estimates in half because "The schedule is too long."

Saying "Keep the project the same, but give me a shorter schedule" makes about as much sense as trying to make a basketball smaller just by squeezing it harder. At best, you'll temporarily squeeze it into a different shape; at worst, you'll deflate it, making it unusable for its intended purpose.

A software project can be squeezed into a different shape, too. Typically the front end gets squeezed first; squeezing the front end of a project pushes work into the back end of a project. When less time is spent in the front end, more defects are created and fewer are removed. The project team not only has to correct all the mistakes it made in the front end, but it has to correct those mistakes at greater cost than if the front-end work had been done correctly in the first place. Unlike squeezing a basketball, squeezing a software project estimate is likely to make the overall project larger instead of deflating it.

If you want to ensure the success of the software project, educate the other project stakeholders about the price of arbitrarily changing cost and schedule estimates without making corresponding changes in the work that needs to be done. If you're an upper manager and you want the development team to cut the schedule in half, be aware that the team won't always assume the things you take for granted. When you tell them to cut the schedule in half, be sure to tell them that it's okay to deliver only half the software, too.

STAGED DELIVERY PLAN

Under the plan recommended in this book, the software is ultimately delivered in stages, with the most important functionality delivered first. Figure 11-1 provides a conceptual overview of staged delivery. (This is the same as Figure 5-2 on page 54.)

Because the most important functionality is delivered first, users' critical needs are met sooner. Staged delivery does not actually reduce the amount of time required to deliver software, but it does reduce the amount of time that *seems* to be required to deliver software. Each staged delivery presents tangible evidence of the project's progress, which can be reassuring if your experience with software consists of projects whose schedules seem to extend into infinity and beyond.

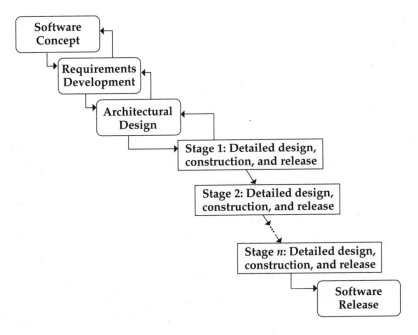

FIGURE 11-1   *Staged delivery. Staged delivery enables the software to be delivered in stages after requirements and the architectural design are developed. It allows the most important functionality to be delivered in the earliest stages.*

Staged delivery cannot happen by accident. It requires a solid architecture, careful management, and detailed technical planning. That work is a good investment in the project because it virtually eliminates the common project risks of late delivery, integration failure, feature creep, and friction between customers, managers, and the project team.

BREAKING THE PROJECT INTO STAGES

In a series of staged deliveries, the first delivery should be the germ of the software that the project team will ultimately deliver. In subsequent releases, the project team adds more capabilities in a carefully planned way. The final software is delivered in the last stage. As Figure 11-1 suggests, within each stage, the project team performs a complete detailed design, construction, and test cycle, and at the end of each stage, it delivers working software. It is important to drive the software to a releasable quality level often, in order to prevent the project from accumulating a host of loose ends that can't be tied up when you actually do want to release the software.

Planning for the first release is unique in that it tends to shake out the bugs in the architecture and requires a certain amount of initial infrastructure building to take place. Be wary of project plans that call for building *all* the infrastructure during Stage 1—such plans reduce the risk-management benefit of the staged delivery approach. If the architecture has been designed well, only the minimum infrastructure work required to deliver Stage 1's functionality should be performed.

As a general goal, try to deliver the software's capabilities in the order of most important to least important. Defining the deliveries in this way forces people to prioritize their work and helps to eliminate gold-plating by deferring delivery of nonessential functionality until later in the project. If you do a good job of prioritizing the releases, the initial deliveries will reduce schedule pressure during the later releases because the users will already have the most critical functionality.

STAGE THEMES

Defining the contents of each stage can give rise to feature-by-feature negotiations that take up a lot of time. A good way to decide which features go into which stages is to define a theme for each stage. Themes are related to the project vision—they are the detailed visions that the team commits to at each stage.

A project team that is developing a word processor might define stage themes such as text editing, basic formatting, advanced formatting, utilities, and integration. Using themes like these raises feature negotiations to a higher level. Themes make it easier to decide which stage to put a particular capability into. Most features will fall naturally into a specific theme. Even if a feature falls into a gray area—for example, automatic list numbering could be considered as advanced formatting or as a utility—you can more easily classify it because you only have to decide which of the two themes is most appropriate. You don't have to consider every stage. Both tables on the facing page show an outline of a Staged Delivery Plan based on stage themes.

When you use themes, the project team probably won't be able to deliver features in exact priority order. Instead, plan to prioritize the themes in order of importance, and then deliver the themes in priority order.

EXAMPLE OF A STAGED DELIVERY PLAN BASED ON STAGE THEMES

Stage	Title	Description
Stage 1	Editing	Text editor is available and includes editing, saving, and printing.
Stage 2	Basic formatting	Character and basic paragraph formatting is available.
Stage 3	Advanced formatting	Advanced formatting is available and includes WYSIWYG page layout and on-screen formatting tools.
Stage 4	Utilities	Utilities are available and include spell checking, thesaurus, grammar checking, hyphenation, and mail merge.
Stage 5	Integration	Full integration with other software is complete.

Theme releases work just as well for in-house software projects as they do for commercial software products. The next table shows an outline of a Staged Delivery Plan for an in-house project.

EXAMPLE OF A STAGED DELIVERY PLAN BASED ON STAGE THEMES

Stage	Title	Description
Stage 1	Database	Billing database is in place, and billing information can be stored and retrieved from the database.
Stage 2	Billing	Standard bills and international bills can be printed, addressed, and so on. Payments can be received.
Stage 3	Networking	Networked data input is complete.
Stage 4	Extended reporting	Management summary reports and analysis reports are complete.
Stage 5	Automation	Unattended monthly processing is available.

The use of themes shouldn't be taken as an invitation to abbreviate release planning. The word processor and billing system examples are just summaries of the themes for each release. The development team will still need to map out exactly which features it plans to deliver during each release. If it doesn't, you won't know exactly what to expect in each staged delivery and you'll lose some of the project-tracking benefit of this approach.

STAGED DELIVERY PLAN LOOK-ALIKES

Some projects follow a percentage approach and plan to deliver software re- leases at 80 percent complete, 90 percent complete, and 100 percent complete. Without a list detailing the contents of each stage, percentages are not sufficient to guide a staged release plan. If a percent target is augmented with the same level of detail as a theme release, using percentages can work acceptably well, although they don't provide the same kind of guidance for deciding what to put into each release that themes do.

Similarly, breaking the project into alpha, beta, and final releases is not actually a staged delivery approach. Rather, it is a plan to deliver feature- complete software at alpha release time with such low quality that three phases are needed to make the software run correctly. This is a costly alter- native to a true staged delivery approach—the project team will spend the alpha, beta, and final release phases correcting defects downstream that could have been corrected more economically upstream.

RELEASING THE RELEASES

The project team doesn't necessarily have to deliver each release to a customer to follow the staged delivery practice. In the case of the word processor described earlier in this chapter, the project team might not release a version to its customer until Stage 3 or 4 or even 5. But it can still use staged delivery as an aid to track progress, coordinate drops to quality assurance, and reduce the risk of integration problems. The project team can get a lot of mileage out of staged releases even if they deliver them only to quality assurance, marketing, and other stakeholders who want to see that the team is making progress.

The frequency with which a project team releases software to custom- ers will depend on how many customers it has and its relationship to them. If it has only a handful of internal customers, the release procedure can be informal and the team can release software as often as every week or so. If the team has hundreds or thousands of customers, the release procedure will need to be much more formal and the team probably shouldn't plan releases more frequently than every two or three months. More frequent external releases will burden the project with external release overhead—disabling features that aren't fully operational, creating release notes, walking through the release procedure, coaching users through installation, and fielding support calls—without significantly lowering the project's technical or management risks.

Each staged release should hit the quality target set for the final software. One benefit of staged releases is that they keep the software's quality from sliding for long periods without detection. Pushing a release out the door without bringing its quality up to the desired level hurts the chances of ever raising the final software's quality to the desired level.

Revising the Staged Delivery Plan

The Staged Delivery Plan should be submitted to change control, reviewed, and then baselined just as other critical project work products are. But this document should not be treated as frozen. The work done during the rest of the project will expose issues that weren't considered during the initial stage planning, and some adjustments to the plan will be needed. At that point, the Staged Delivery Plan should be updated to reflect the revised plan through use of the change control process.

Ongoing Planning Activities

Final preparations time is about focused planning, so it is important to step back from the day-to-day activities of the project and take a fresh look at the plans that were developed earlier.

Risk Management

Explicit risk-management activities that were initiated at the beginning of the project should continue throughout the project. As project tasks become better defined, so do the risks. The Top 10 Risks List should have been updated several times by now; during the final preparations period, look for new risks that might not have been apparent before. Look for risks associated with cost, available computing resources, available personnel, and questionable technical aspects of the project.

Many of the practices recommended in this book have been selected for their ability to control the most common, most critical project risks. Use of the Change Control Plan and the Software Integration Procedure, regular refinement of project estimates, and the staged delivery approach all reduce project risks, although they are not primarily risk-management activities.

Project Vision

Is the project vision still appropriate for the project? In some instances, so much is learned about the project during requirements development that the vision doesn't really match the project anymore. Project team members might all agree that the original vision is no longer valid, but they won't all synchronize their work on the same new vision unless a specific new vision is given official standing. Check the vision statement and, if necessary, revise it so that it can provide direction throughout stage planning, architecture, and detailed design and implementation.

Decision-Making Authority

Check whether the decision-making authority identified during preliminary planning is clear about the project plans and goals, including the Change Control Plan and preliminary estimates. If the decision-making authority is not aware of or in agreement with project plans, be sure any issues are settled before detailed design and implementation begin.

Personnel

The period of final preparations is also an appropriate time to step back from personnel issues and to check that the project team is healthy. Here are a few guidelines for assessing the well-being of the project's personnel.

- Project morale should be high. If it isn't, find out why not and fix it.

- The project should not have any problem team members. If any team members are causing problems, remove them *now* before they further damage the team's morale and while there's still time to bring in new team members without hurting existing team members' productivity.

- The way the team is organized should be working. If it isn't working, change it.

- If some team members have demonstrated weaknesses, provide supplementary training.

- Check whether it will be possible to recruit the remaining project members that the Software Development Plan calls for. If not, add that as a risk to the Top 10 Risks List.

◆   Check whether the project is registering a strong positive in its people-aware management accountability. Is the project running in such a way that the project's human resources will emerge from the project worth more to the organization rather than less? If the project is burning people up before implementation starts, the project is headed for trouble.

UPDATING THE SOFTWARE DEVELOPMENT PLAN

The Software Development Plan created during preliminary planning should be revised and updated to reflect the planning that has been done during this final preparations period. The revised plan should be reviewed and approved by the project manager, development team, quality assurance people, and documentation team, and then it should be placed under change control.

Survival Check

👍 The project team creates its first estimate after preliminary requirements development is complete.

💣 Estimates do not account for normal activities such as holidays, weekends, and vacations.

💣 Developers don't believe the estimates are realistic.

👍 Estimates are updated after detailed requirements development and again after architectural design.

👍 The project has a Staged Delivery Plan that organizes the stages into theme releases.

💣 The stages are not defined in detail.

👍 The project's risk-management, vision, decision-making, and personnel plans are up-to-date.

👍 The project's Software Development Plan is up-to-date and is being followed.

III

SUCCEEDING BY STAGES

12
Beginning-of-Stage Planning

Beginning-of-stage planning, which maps out a detailed course of action for a stage, is performed at the start of each staged delivery cycle. The project team creates an Individual Stage Plan that describes how to conduct detailed design, coding, technical reviews, tests, integration, and other activities during the stage. The most labor-intensive planning activity is the creation of a list of miniature milestones, which helps the team track progress throughout the stage. Creating these milestones requires a lot of work, but the activity is worthwhile because of the considerable status visibility and risk reduction it provides.

Each stage in a project using the staged delivery approach is essentially a miniature project. Each stage includes planning, design, construction, testing, and preparation for release. Members of the software industry have often observed that a series of small projects seems to involve less risk than one large one—staged delivery is a means of turning one large, risky project into a series of smaller projects, each of which involves less risk.

WHY IS STAGE PLANNING NEEDED?

A client of mine put the second version of one of its software products out to bid. One vendor proposed to deliver the product in 5 months. The second vendor proposed to deliver the product in 9 months. That vendor expressed concerns about the project's scope, which accounted for the longer schedule estimate. The vendor prioritized the product's requirements and proposed to deliver a release of the product that contained the highest priority improvements within 3 months. It planned to follow the first release with a second release within 6 months and a final release within 9 months. This second vendor noted that my client's customers were clamoring loudest for the functionality that would be delivered during Stage 1 and proposed that my client ship the Stage 1 release as a version 1.5 product. After evaluating the proposals, my client decided that the risks related to the project's scope were not a serious problem and selected the first vendor and its 5-month plan.

As it turned out, everyone should have been as concerned about the scope of the project as the second vendor was. The selected vendor missed the first few milestone dates by 100 to 200 percent. Six months into the project, the vendor reestimated that it would complete the project in 9 months; 9 months into the project it estimated it would finish in 12; by 12 months, the project was beset by quality problems, and no one believed the vendor's estimates anymore. In the meantime, 12 months passed and my client didn't have a version 2.0 or even a version 1.5 to release to its customers.

Shaky estimates are facts of life in software projects, and staged deliveries help to minimize the damage shaky estimates can cause. If my client had mapped out a 3-release Stage Plan, it might not have received its first release in the promised 3 months, but it probably would have received it in 4 months. With a staged delivery plan, my client could have released the most important new functionality to its customers after 4 months rather than emerging from 12 months of development work empty handed.

Staged releases force development teams to "converge" the software—bring it to a releasable state—multiple times over the course of a project. Converging the software reduces the risks of low quality, lack of status visibility, and schedule overruns, which should provide as much incentive as anyone needs to be enthusiastic about planning a little at the beginning of each stage.

STAGE PLANNING OVERVIEW

During each stage, the project is guided globally by the planning described in the Software Development Plan. It is guided locally by a Stage Plan that is created at the beginning of the stage. After each Stage Plan is written, it is added to the Software Development Plan. Unless the project is quite large, each Stage Plan should be only a few pages long.

Milestones, schedules, and task assignments should be described for the following activities in the Stage Plan:

◆   Requirements updates

◆   Detailed design

◆   Construction

◆   Test case creation

◆   User documentation updates

◆   Technical reviews

◆   Defect corrections

◆   Technical coordination

◆   Risk management

◆   Project tracking

◆   Integration and release

◆   End-of-stage wrap-up

Each of these activities is performed during each stage. This section provides details about them.

REQUIREMENTS UPDATES

In the early stages, the requirements to be implemented during the stages should be exactly what the project team specified during prototyping and requirements development. During later stages, improved understanding of the software being built, changing market conditions, and other factors may necessitate changes to requirements. Time should be allocated at the beginning of each stage—especially the beginnings of the later stages—to evaluate possible changes to requirements.

DETAILED DESIGN

Near the beginning of each stage, developers flesh out the detailed design so that it adequately supports the software construction that will be done during the stage. If detailed design work uncovers flaws in the architecture, the project team revises the architecture using the change control procedure.

CONSTRUCTION

After developers complete the detailed design for a stage, they code the software to be delivered during the stage. Coding is supported by a practice called "the daily build and smoke test process" (which is explained in Chapter 14, "Construction"). Detailed design flows easily into coding because on most software projects, the developer who creates the detailed design for a specific part of the software also writes the code for that part.

TEST CASE CREATION

At the same time the developers are working on a stage's construction, testers should create the full set of test cases needed to test the functionality developed during the stage. Test cases can be constructed in parallel with the code because they can be based partially on the detailed User Interface Prototype created during requirements development and partially on the code that developers informally turn over to testing before the code is officially declared complete. (Details of this practice are described in Chapter 14, "Construction.")

USER DOCUMENTATION UPDATES

The User Manual/Requirements Specification is updated to describe the as-built software. Help files and other kinds of end-user documentation are created.

TECHNICAL REVIEWS

Developers participate in design and code reviews. Design and code reviews begin in earnest during the post-architecture period, and the Stage Plan should allow time for them.

DEFECT CORRECTION

Developers correct the defects uncovered by testing and reviews. One of the critical advantages of staged delivery is its ability to minimize the risk of low quality by forcing the software's quality to a releasable level by the end of each stage. The defects detected during a particular stage must be corrected during that stage and the corrections must be verified by testing, by technical reviews, or by both to mitigate the risk of low quality.

TECHNICAL COORDINATION

Every project requires coordination between developers and testers, and the schedule should allow time for that coordination. Managers of large projects will need to coordinate the activities of different groups of developers. Developers typically also need to be available to explain their implementations to technical writers and to review the technical writers' documents. When the approach described in this book is used, the project has already created a full-fledged User Interface Prototype and User Manual/Requirements Specification, so the amount of coordination required on the project will be less than on many other projects.

Some changes to requirements and the user interface are inevitable as the software is developed in detail. Developers will need to be available to explain those changes to testers and technical writers.

RISK MANAGEMENT

Stage planning should be risk driven. The project manager should review the project's current Top 10 Risks List and determine whether the current project plan adequately addresses the current risks to the project. Many times, the top 10 risks at the end of a stage will have changed from the risks at the beginning of the stage, and different plans will be required. The "Survival Check" at the end of each chapter in this book provides a list of warning signs to look for throughout the project and particularly at the end of each stage.

PROJECT TRACKING

Tracking completed activities is the major management task during all stages. The section in this chapter called "Miniature Milestones" discusses project tracking in detail.

INTEGRATION AND RELEASE

At the end of each stage, the development team brings the software to a releasable state. Developers integrate the code for that release. They correct defects. They raise the software's fit and finish to release quality. (When I say "fit and finish," I mean that the software's install program works, the context-sensitive help displays the correct help topics, and so on.)

At this point the software may be released in whatever way makes the most business sense:

◆ It can simply be declared to be "released," the team can celebrate its accomplishment, and work can begin immediately on the next stage.

◆ It can be released to specific in-house users, external users, or both.

◆ It can be released generally to in-house users for their review and evaluation.

◆ It can be released to the whole group of in-house users, external users, or both.

The decision about how widely to distribute the release should be based on business considerations rather than on technical considerations. The software's technical quality at the end of each stage should make it possible to release the software to virtually anyone. But the software might not contain enough new functionality to warrant distributing it widely, or the project team might not want to absorb the cost and schedule overhead associated with managing an external release.

However, if external users are eager for new functionality and the development team has organized releases by priority, distributing staged releases to external users as the releases become available might be a good business decision.

Whether ultimately released to users or not, the software should always be released to the quality assurance group. It doesn't do the project any good to have the software declared fit for release unless that claim is verified independently of the project team.

End-of-Stage Wrap-Up

At the end of a stage, the project team should pause to review its progress to date and make any necessary course corrections. The project team should identify practices that have worked and those that should change so that the project will work better. By the end of each stage, the project team will have developed a deeper understanding of the software it is implementing and can create increasingly accurate cost and schedule estimates.

Miniature Milestones

A critical management activity during each stage is active progress tracking. The plan for each stage needs to lay the groundwork for tracking progress; the way to do that is to create a set of detailed milestones, or miniature milestones, by which the project manager can assess the project's status.

Miniature milestones are targets that developers and other project members have to meet frequently—at least once a week, preferably more often. "Daily" is probably the smallest practical milestone size. Each milestone is "binary," which means it is either *done* or *not done*: it is not "90 percent done." Because these milestones are small, some people call them "inch-pebbles." Other people call them "microstones."

To understand why milestones need to be binary to be useful, put yourself in this analogous situation: Suppose you estimated that you needed 100 cans of spray paint to paint the side of your house. And suppose that you're interrupted every 30 seconds and throw whatever can you're using into a big pile of spray paint cans. Each time you resume painting, you simply pick up the most convenient can. After an hour or so, someone comes up and asks how much paint you have left. At that point, you'll have a big pile of cans in which some of the cans are completely empty, some are completely full, and most are partially full. You will have a hard time estimating the amount of paint remaining.

If instead you are careful to use the same can until it runs out of paint, and to keep the empty cans separate from the full cans, you'll know to within 1 can of paint out of 100 cans (1 percent) how much paint you have left. The same principle applies to software project management. If you know for certain that each task is either done or not done, you have pretty good information about how much work has been completed and how much work remains.

In addition to their project tracking benefit, miniature milestones help the team to focus on the most important tasks. When only long-term milestones are used, the developers can easily lose a day here or a week there—people spend time on detours that seem interesting or productive in some vague sense but that fail to move the project forward.

———◆———

"How does a project get to be a year late?...
One day at a time."
—Frederick P. Brooks

———◆———

When short-term milestones are used, you will find out almost immediately whether the project is going to have problems meeting its overall schedule: if it starts missing milestones, it's going to have problems. That early warning gives the project team an early opportunity to recalibrate the schedule or adjust the project plan in other ways.

CREATING A COMPLETE MILESTONE LIST

Be sure that the list of milestones includes every task needed to release the software. The most common source of software estimation errors is overlooking necessary tasks. Do not allow developers to keep a list of "off schedule" work in their heads—or on their whiteboards, or on sticky notes, or in any place other than the official schedule. I worked on one project with a developer who swore he was "almost done" and then "completely done" with his assignments. When we got close enough to the release date that we could plan out the rest of the project step by step, this developer acknowledged that he had about six weeks of "little clean-up projects" that needed to be done. Not surprisingly, he had also severely underestimated how much work he had left to do, and the real work remaining turned out to be closer to four months than six weeks.

Was the schedule problem the developer's fault? Partly. But his manager could have prevented the problem by insisting on more detailed reporting—and his manager should have insisted on that.

Insist that every task be included on the milestone list: detailed design, coding, reviews, correction of defects detected during reviews, integration of developers' work, cleaning up quick-and-dirty fixes—that is, *everything*. When the last milestone is marked "complete," the project should be complete.

This particular risk of incomplete task lists is addressed at multiple levels by the approach described in this book. Missing tasks should be flushed out during detailed design work. If they aren't flushed out then, they'll be flushed out during creation of miniature milestones.

———◆———

Like all good software project plans, this book's approach is based on the reality that mistakes will be made throughout the project. Project success depends on positioning the project team to detect and correct these mistakes quickly and easily.

———◆———

ACHIEVING DESIRED QUALITY

Performing technical reviews on every work product helps to ensure that both the letter and the spirit of the miniature milestone practice is followed. Technical reviews reduce the chance that a developer will be able to claim work is complete when it is not. If a module is supposed to be "done," it will be reviewed. The review will then determine whether it is really done.

Technical reviews also help prevent the insidious accumulation of quality assurance work, which is a common risk on projects. When developers declare code to be "done" and the technical review shows the code to be of high quality, you can have a clear picture of how much of the project's work has been completed and how much remains. Without technical reviews, a team can too easily declare low quality work to be done. Defects accumulate until the end of the project, hurting status visibility. Defect correction work grows, unnoticed, until the software is functionally complete and a seemingly endless stream of quality problems prevents its release.

A more subtle and damaging effect of allowing low quality work to be declared done is that, in addition to covertly deferring work to the end of the project, it actually *increases* the total effort required to raise the software's quality to any particular level. Because of all the possible interactions among components, debugging three or four low quality components and their interactions is more difficult than debugging each low quality component in isolation. The consequences for projects are dramatic. A typical medium-size project might have 1000 to 2000 routines and 250 to 500 modules or more.

——◆——

*If quality assurance work is deferred to the end of
the project, developers are faced with debugging
not just interactions among three or four low
quality components. They're faced with debugging
interactions among hundreds or thousands
of low quality components.*

——◆——

Once you understand this concept, you can also understand why months can pass between the time a program seems largely complete and the time it attains a releasable quality level. If the quality of each of a program's components is really poor, it might be impossible—practically speaking—for that software ever to achieve a releasable quality level.

HOW FAR OUT TO DEFINE MINIATURE MILESTONES

In defining miniature milestones, the project team plans a route toward the next major landmark. It maps out a detailed route only for the part of the terrain that it can see from its current vantage point. The team should create miniature milestones twice during each stage:

- The team should define a first set of milestones to get it through detailed design.

- When the team finishes detailed design, it should define a second set of milestones to get them through the software release, which occurs at the end of the stage.

Defining miniature milestones will take time, but many people who have used this practice feel that once they have defined the milestones, their work is already half done.

MINIATURE MILESTONES ON SMALL PROJECTS

Small project teams sometimes think they don't need to define miniature milestones because their projects are small and therefore require less management. But the relative risk of cost and schedule overruns on a small project is the same as on a large project. A one-month overrun on a one-month project is less noticeable than a one-year overrun on a one-year project, but the proportion of the overrun is the same. The amount of effort needed to use the miniature milestone practice is also proportional to the size of the project. Miniature milestones provide just as much visibility and control benefit on small projects as on large projects.

POLITICAL CONSIDERATIONS

Some developers view miniature milestones as micromanagement, and that's what they are. But not all micromanagement is bad. And this is not the kind of micromanagement that developers dislike, but a truly effective means of tracking progress. Because more specifically, miniature milestones are a kind of micro–project tracking.

People who don't fully understand their jobs will feel threatened by the miniature milestone practice because it will show that they don't understand the details of their work. If the project manager handles their objections diplomatically, learning to work to a miniature milestone schedule can be an educational experience for them. Project members will become skilled at mapping out their tasks using milestones. They will learn how to plan their work systematically and will feel increasingly in control of their work.

To minimize political repercussions, the project manager should let people define their own miniature milestones. The miniature milestone practice doesn't give the project manager the right to control every detail of people's work; it merely requires that people tell the manager what those details are. After that, project members should keep the project manager apprised of their progress by entering it into the publicly available project plan.

Be sure miniature milestones are set up early in the project. As with other aspects of project control, it's easiest to exercise more control in the beginning and relax control as the project progresses. As Barry Boehm and Rony Ross say, "Hard-soft works better than soft-hard." Expect some initial resistance, but beware of the developer who resists miniature milestones at all costs. Such a developer is literally out of control—you'll never have a clear sense of what the developer is working on or the status of the work. That developer's attempt to avoid accountability at all costs gives you the best hint you're likely to get about that developer's contribution to the project.

What to Do If the Project Misses Its Miniature Milestones

If the miniature milestone plan is realistic and the project team maintains its focus, the team should be able to stay on schedule by working normal hours and a small amount of what Fergus O'Connell calls surgical overtime—a few extra hours in specific places to meet specific miniature milestones.

Missed miniature milestones provide early warning that the project as a whole is at risk of failing to meet its schedule. If you find that the project is missing milestones frequently, don't try to catch up by having the development team work harder to meet each milestone. The project will just get further behind.

If a developer is staying focused but has kept to a milestone schedule only by working extraordinary amounts of overtime, that developer's schedule should be recalibrated. That developer does not have any schedule cushion, and any task that's been underestimated more severely than others will blow the whole schedule out of the water.

That developer also needs to be given enough time to be able to quit making rushed, careless decisions that ultimately make the project take longer. Working smart and hard is OK. Working hard at the expense of working smart is not.

You have several options when miniature milestones are not being met. You can recalibrate the schedule so that the developer can meet deadlines by working normal eight-hour days. To do this, multiply the schedule for that developer's remaining miniature milestone dates by the size of the schedule slip so far. You can also trim the software's feature set, clear away distractions so that developers can focus better, reassign parts of the project to developers who seem to be meeting their milestones easily, or take other corrective actions.

Stage Planning and Management Styles

Some project managers will object to the hands-on management approach described in this chapter. They prefer a hands-off management style and say they don't need to incur the overhead of delivering in stages, tracking progress in detail, evaluating risks frequently, or replanning automatically when conditions change.

When thinking about hands-on and hands-off styles, realize that "hands-off management" can refer to keeping hands off the people working on the project or to keeping hands off the project itself. Keeping hands

184

off the people on the project might be the best choice. Effective project leadership certainly requires a qualitative understanding of the needs of the specific people on a project.

But keeping hands off the project itself sets the project up for failure. Hands-off management allows costs that are 50 to 200 times too high to creep into a project. Major schedule slips go undetected until the night before the software is supposed to be released. Critical risks can go unnoticed until it's too late to address them effectively. The problems arising from hands-off project management ultimately lead to projects failing that could easily have succeeded.

Effective software project management benefits from the systematic application of hands-on practices. Some of the most effective practices require hard work, but in exchange, these practices produce exceptional risk reduction, status visibility, and schedule control. Careful stage planning, including the use of miniature milestones, is one such practice.

Survival Check

 Planning is conducted at the beginning of each stage to prepare for that stage's activities.

 Stage planning includes requirements review, detailed design, coding and code reviews, test case creation, user documentation updates, in-stage defect correction, technical coordination, integration and release, risk management, project tracking, and other important activities.

 The project team creates a set of miniature milestones to aid in tracking progress throughout the stage.

   The list of miniature milestones does not include all activities.

   The project is not actually tracked against the list of miniature milestones.

 The project manager adopts a hands-on approach to the project.

13 *Detailed Design*

The detailed design activity during each stage extends the design work begun during architecture, addressing many of the same issues but in more detail. The amount of detailed design work required depends on the project's size and the developers' expertise. Reviews of detailed designs provide significant quality and cost benefits. Detailed design during Stage 1 of the project requires some special work, such as verifying the quality of the architecture.

D uring detailed design for a particular stage, the developers focus on designing all the specific parts of the system that will be delivered during that stage. Some consideration of work to be done during later stages might be needed, but if the architecture was crafted well, developers will be able to create detailed designs without thinking very much about the parts of the software that will be developed in later stages. They can assume that if their work follows the architecture, it will be compatible with later work.

ARCHITECTURE REVISITED

During detailed design, the development team will work in several design areas that were first explored during the architecture phase.

PROGRAM ORGANIZATION

At architecture time, designers were concerned with the program's organization at the system level. At detailed design time, they are concerned with the program's organization at the class and routine level.

REUSE ANALYSIS

Developers again investigate the possibility of reusing existing components and commercially available components in their designs, but this time that investigation will explore reuse at a more detailed level—individual classes and routines instead of whole application frameworks and subsystem-level class libraries.

REQUIREMENTS RESOLUTION

As I mentioned in Chapter 8, "Requirements Development," project teams sometimes need to leave a few requirements unresolved at requirements time. However, any requirements affecting a particular staged release *must* be resolved during the detailed design phase of that release. If the requirements cannot be resolved, they can be deferred until the detailed design phase of a later stage, but the project leadership should be aware that at this point in the project, significant effort and schedule penalties will be incurred by remaining indecisive.

REQUIREMENTS TRACEABILITY

Detailed designs need to be responsive to all relevant requirements just as the architecture did. This is sometimes called "requirements flow-down," because requirements flow from requirements to architecture to detailed design to code and test cases. Effective work on requirements traceability is one of the activities most critical to the success of a project at this point. I'll have more to say about this later in the chapter.

CONSTRUCTION PLAN

Developers should generate a comprehensive construction plan and a list of miniature milestones for the construction phase of a particular stage. If you get through the detailed design phase and developers tell you that they can't create a comprehensive plan, you should be very concerned—you've got a key warning sign that their detailed designs are not thorough enough. Developers need to continue working on the detailed designs until they can create miniature milestones for construction.

CORRECTION OF DEFECTS IN THE ARCHITECTURE

Even when the architecture is outstanding and its reviewers have been diligent, it will still contain a few defects that will be flushed out during detailed design. Developers will discover gaps that need to be filled in, inconsistencies that need to be resolved, and spurious elements that can be eliminated. This will be less true during detailed design for the first stage because it follows on the heels of architecture. It will be more true during detailed design for the later stages when the development team has worked more with the architecture and has a better understanding of its strengths and weaknesses.

HOW MUCH DETAILED DESIGN DOES A PROJECT NEED?

The amount of design work and the formality of that work depend on two factors: the expertise of the project's developers and the difficulty of the project. Figure 13-1 on the following page illustrates the point.

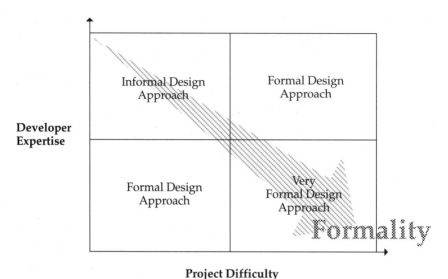

FIGURE 13-1   *The relationship between detailed design formality, project difficulty, and developer expertise. The less experienced the developers and the more difficult the project, the more formality is needed in detailed design.*

As the figure suggests, when the project has expert developers and is a simple project (one in which construction will take only a couple of months), the detailed design work can be informal. Design work can proceed in parallel with construction, and developers can probably combine many construction and design activities.

When a project has inexperienced developers and is difficult (because the team anticipates that construction will take more than a couple of months, or because the project employs unfamiliar technology, demands high reliability, or explores a new application area), the project team should adopt a formal design approach in which each component of the system is designed and reviewed before it is constructed. At this level of formality, you should expect to see module diagrams for every class in the system and textual descriptions of each routine. All but the most trivial routines should be written out in pseudocode and reviewed before they are implemented.

The project cases that fall in the middle—expert developers working on a difficult project or inexperienced developers working on a simple project—usually call for some design formality, and I think it is best to err on the side of too much formality rather than too little, for several reasons.

One reason is that it can be terribly difficult to assess the expertise of a developer with whom you are unfamiliar. I consulted on a project in which the client had contracted with an expert in object oriented design to help the client tackle its first major object oriented project. This expert claimed to have five years of experience in object oriented development work, and his references had made him sound like he could walk on water. When we finished requirements work and began working on the design, the project manager said to the expert, "Why don't you take over the design meeting and guide us through the first steps of creating an object oriented design?"

The expert's response was, "This is the part of the project where my clients get kind of nervous because I don't really know how to explain what I do. I just know that what I do always works out." Clearly, that raised a red flag, and it turned out that, in spite of his years of experience, the object oriented "expert" knew only as much about object oriented design as the team members who had read a few magazine articles.

If you err on the side of too much formality, the team will create an effective design, but the formal steps the team takes—creating design diagrams, writing pseudocode, and reviewing the detailed design separately from the code—will add overhead to the project.

However, if you err on the side of too little formality, you risk basing construction and testing work on low quality and error-prone designs. That will give rise to a substantial amount of rework later in the project and increase the schedule and budget risks.

———◆———

The smart money is on too much design formality
rather than too little.

———◆———

Successful projects look for ways to trade small increases in overhead for large decreases in project risk, and adding formality to the design process is a classic (and effective) way to do that. You could even question whether the extra work performed in the formal approach is really "overhead." After all, it results in the creation of documentation that will undoubtedly be useful to generations of developers who maintain the system and that will quite possibly be useful to the generation of developers who are working on the system right now.

TECHNICAL REVIEWS

After the author of the design for a particular component thinks the design is complete, the design is reviewed. Each member of a review team will review the design, and then the team will hold a review meeting to discuss its findings.

The most efficient size for a review team is two or three reviewers other than the design's author. Numerous software engineering studies have found that different reviewers find different kinds of defects, so use at least two reviewers or you will almost certainly leave major defects undetected. The project will probably detect more defects when more than three reviewers examine the designs, but the cost-effectiveness drops fast.

This pre-meeting review work is essential because most of the potential defects will be detected during these reviews. If the project team is forced to choose between conducting the pre-meeting review work or holding the actual review meeting, the team should cancel the review meeting and ask reviewers to report their findings individually to the design's author.

The ideal amount of material reviewed in a design review meeting varies from one organization to another. The project team will learn over time how much material works best. To start, the reviewers should try reviewing the designs for a single class, a handful of routines, or no more than about 100 lines of pseudocode at one meeting. Reviewing much less than that will fragment the reviewers' time too much; reviewing much more will tend to overload the reviewers and hurt the quality of their reviews.

DETECTING FUNCTIONAL DEFECTS

During the review meeting, each detailed design component should be reviewed for these characteristics:

- *Correctness.* Will the design work as intended?

- *Completeness.* Is the design adequate for all its intended purposes?

- *Understandability.* Can the design be understood easily by others?

Complex designs are correlated with increased numbers of errors, so a design should be made as simple as possible to avoid errors during a program's initial development. Moreover, the benefits of focusing on understandability extends far beyond initial development. Studies of software maintenance have found that maintenance programmers spend more time trying to understand the original program than they spend modifying it.

Since the average program is maintained by 10 generations of maintenance programmers, the short time spent focusing on understandability during a design review is time well spent.

DETECTING REQUIREMENTS DEFECTS

The design is also evaluated for traceability to requirements. That is, the design is reviewed in order to determine whether all necessary requirements have been addressed and whether the design contains elements that are superfluous because they do not respond to any requirements.

Missing Requirements

Detection of omitted requirements is critical because it helps to avoid the error of forgetting to design for all requirements. When the design overlooks a requirement, the system will need to be retrofitted to address that requirement later in the project at greater cost.

Unrequired Functionality

Detection of functionality beyond what is required is also critical because unrequired functionality quickly increases a project's cost and schedule. The addition of a small amount of extra functionality might seem to be a minor matter, but the addition of a minor feature—even one invisible to the user— can incur some or all of the following penalties:

- Additional coding, testing, and debugging time
- Additional complexity, which makes the system inherently more error-prone
- Additional system test cases
- Additional defects to be detected, corrected, and tracked in the defect tracking system
- Additional user documentation
- Additional user support training
- Additional user support e-mail and telephone calls
- Additional functionality that must be supported by future versions of the program

I once reviewed the designs for a program that performed sophisticated analytical functions. The analytical operations involved were inherently complex; this system would be the first of its kind in the world. The design and implementation *at its simplest* would be a major challenge.

The project team decided that it would be cool if the different components of the system could interact "asynchronously." Coordinating the processing of two asynchronous parts of a program is pretty complicated. Apply this complexity to hundreds of places throughout a program, and this "cool" (and unrequired) feature probably increased the effort needed to implement the already-complicated system by 50 to 100 percent. The asynchronous capability was essentially invisible to the people who were paying for the system, and I have no doubt that if they had been given the choice, the customers would not have thought that feature warranted a 50 to 100 percent higher price tag.

In addition to its cost consequences, code that isn't required can have disastrous consequences for the software itself. The Ariane 5 rocket, which exploded on its maiden voyage in 1996, failed because of some alignment code that was not specifically required for the Ariane 5. That code had been used in previous models of the Ariane and had simply not been removed from the Ariane 5.

During detailed design, a project's cost can be cut in half or doubled, and the software can be made more or less reliable, depending on whether the development team consistently looks for ways to simplify the software's design or ways to make it more comprehensive, complex, and technically interesting. When the projectwide implications are considered, few unrequired design features are cool enough to justify their end-to-end costs.

———◆———

Because of their ability to catch and eliminate overly expensive and unreliable feature implementations, technical reviews can pay for themselves many times over.

———◆———

REVIEWING FOR PROJECT OBJECTIVES

Design reviews are a time when developers can discuss ways of making a design responsive to the project's objectives. If the project objective is to deliver the software at least cost, reviewers are often able to point out refinements that will make the design cheaper to implement. If the objective is ultimate adaptability, portability, or something else, reviewers can find better ways to accomplish those objectives too.

The vision defined early in the project will become critically important during this detailed design stage. A clear vision will provide guidance during design reviews, which will move the software toward its objective. An unclear vision cannot provide any such guidance, and reviews will not be able to improve the software.

CROSS-TRAINING

A benefit of design reviews is the insurance they provide against the what-if-our-key-developer-Joe-gets-hit-by-a-beer-truck syndrome. The two or more reviewers who have reviewed Joe's designs will be familiar with Joe's work and capable of stepping into his place. Joe's untimely demise will be a cause for mourning, but not for canceling the project. Design reviews provide similar insurance against the what-if-Joe-turns-out-to-be-a-complete-jerk-but-we're-totally-dependent-on-him syndrome. Think of reviews as a kind of "jerk insurance."

REVIEWS AND PRODUCTIVITY

The savings potential from defect detection conducted during reviews is huge—about 60 percent of all defects usually exist by design time, and the project team should try to eliminate them by then. A decision to not focus on defect detection at detailed design time amounts to a decision to postpone defect detection and correction until later in the project, when detection and correction will be much more expensive and time-consuming.

Because they can be used early in the development cycle, technical reviews—especially the kind of review known as inspections—have been found to produce net schedule savings of 10 to 30 percent. One study of large programs even found that each hour spent on inspections avoided an average of 33 hours of maintenance, and that inspections were up to 20 times more efficient than testing.

Detailed Design Documents

Developers should create some kind of Detailed Design Document for each program component. Depending on the size of the project, each Detailed Design Document might cover a class, a group of classes, or a subsystem. On most medium-sized projects (the size this book discusses), it is appropriate to have a Detailed Design Document for each subsystem.

These documents do not need to be especially formal. Depending on the level of formality the project decides is appropriate, they can be collections of loose-leaf design diagrams; combinations of design diagrams and pseudocode; or small documents that contain introductions, design diagrams, pseudocode, requirements traceability matrixes, and other relevant materials.

Regardless of how formal the detailed designs are, each Detailed Design Document should be placed under change control after its corresponding design has passed its review. Some of the work products placed under change control—such as requirements, architecture, and coding standards—will be updated only infrequently. Because changes to those work products have such far-reaching cost and schedule implications, the change control process should make them difficult to change. Other work products—such as source code—need to be updated more frequently, and the change control process for them should be more streamlined. Detailed Design Documents written at the subsystem level will be updated many times throughout the course of a project as the subsystems are fleshed out through each stage. The change control process applied to documents at this level should resemble the change control process for source code more than the change control processes for upstream work products.

Special Considerations for Stage 1 of the Project

During Stage 1 of a project, some special considerations may apply to the design activity. On smaller projects or on projects where very experienced developers are involved, architecture is sometimes rolled into Stage 1. On medium and medium-to-large projects, architecture should be completed before staged development begins, but the first stage should still explore the viability of and risks to the system's architecture.

Understanding the best way to explore the architecture's risks depends on understanding the difference between "horizontal" and "vertical" slices of a system. Suppose you have an analytical system that generates five graphs. You can define sets of graphs, and you can edit, print, save, and retrieve them. A "horizontal" slice of the system would explore the same bit of functionality for each of the five graphs. For example, such a slice might explore the printing of rough versions of each of the five graphs. A "vertical" slice of the system would explore functionality for only one graph, but it would explore the bare-bones top-to-bottom functionality for that graph, including editing, printing, saving, and retrieving.

If the project faces a strong technological risk (that is, the project is working with leading-edge technology, development tools that are unfamiliar to the development team, or both), it should focus on a vertical slice of the system during Stage 1. That will allow the team to exercise each of the technologies involved and verify that they are compatible with one another in the way the architecture intended. If the project doesn't face a strong technological risk (that is, it is working with well-understood tools in a well-understood environment), the part of the system the team builds during the first stage must force it to exercise and explore all the important interfaces and interactions among subsystems. Most often, the first-stage implementation should capture about 80 percent of the breadth of the system and 20 percent of the depth.

Developers should address the most difficult parts of the system first. They don't need to drive those parts all the way to completion, but they should drive them far enough to expose all the significant risks and be sure that they have detailed plans for addressing each of those risks.

Survival Check

 The project team creates the Detailed Design Document for each subsystem, which drives the architectural considerations down to a detailed level and places them under change control.

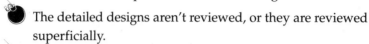 The detailed designs aren't reviewed, or they are reviewed superficially.

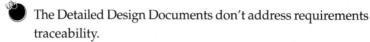 The Detailed Design Documents don't address requirements traceability.

 The degree of formality of the detailed design work seems well-suited to the size of the project and expertise of the developers.

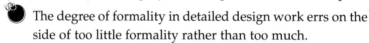 The degree of formality in detailed design work errs on the side of too little formality rather than too much.

 Detailed design reviews focus on finding functional defects, requirements mismatches, and ways in which the project's objectives can be better satisfied.

 The detailed design created during Stage 1 of the project explores potential problems in the architecture.

14 *Construction*

Construction is an exciting time, during which the development team brings the software to life. If the activities preceding construction have been conducted effectively, construction will be a harmonious, industrious time during which developers steadily add functionality to the system by building and smoke testing it each day. During construction, the successful project team becomes increasingly vigilant about finding ways to make the software simpler and to control changes to it. Progress will be highly visible as the project manager monitors key progress indicators, including miniature milestones, defects, the Top 10 Risks List, and the system itself.

During construction, developers begin breathing life into the software by creating the source code that becomes the working computer program. Each developer fills in gaps in the detailed designs from the detailed design phase, creates source code, unit tests and debugs the source code, and integrates the source code with the project's main build.

On a well-run project, the steadily accumulating functionality during construction gives the whole project a lift. The project spins up to a high-performance hum as developers build on each other's contributions, and managers and users grow increasingly confident in the system as they witness the daily accumulation of new functionality.

Construction can be the most enjoyable phase of a software project or the most contentious. This chapter describes how to keep it productive and fun.

SOURCE CODE QUALITY

The way the software is initially constructed has a tremendous impact on the lifetime costs of a system. Consistent application of detailed coding techniques makes the difference between a Rube Goldberg contraption and a polished, correct, and informative program. Such detailed techniques must be applied as the code is initially constructed, because it's virtually impossible to go back later and retrofit the thousands of picky details that spell the difference between an extendable program and an unmaintainable failure.

CODING STANDARD

One of the keys to creating a polished program instead of a Rube Goldberg contraption is having a Coding Standard. The goal of a Coding Standard is to make the whole program look more like a blanket made of a single material than a patchwork quilt made of mismatched scraps. As the project progresses, giving the source code a common look and feel helps developers read each other's code. When the original developers leave the project and new developers take over the software, the new developers will have an easier time understanding the code if it all follows a consistent style.

The Coding Standard typically addresses several areas:

- Layout of classes, modules, routines, and code within routines
- Commenting of classes, modules, routines, and code within routines
- Variable names

- Function names, including names for common operations such as getting and setting values within a class or module
- Maximum length of a routine in lines of source code
- Maximum number of routines within a class
- Degree of complexity allowed, including restrictions on the use of the Goto statement, logical tests, loop nesting, and so on
- Code-level enforcements of architectural standards for memory management, error processing, string storage, and so on
- Versions of tools and libraries to be used
- Conventions for use of tools and libraries
- Naming conventions for source code files
- Source code directory structure for developer machines, build machines, and source code control tools
- Source code file contents (for example, one C++ class per file)
- Ways to indicate incomplete code (for example, with "TBD" comments)

Within an organization, most of the content of a Coding Standard should remain the same from project to project, at least for projects that use the same programming language. The main parts that will vary will be the parts that deal with enforcement of each project's specific architectural approach.

The best coding standards are short, usually less than 25 pages. Trying to standardize every single aspect of the project is pointless—developers won't be able to remember the standards and won't be able to follow them.

Creation of coding standards can be surprisingly contentious, but really the specific details of the convention matter less than the extent to which the convention is followed. A convention's main contribution to a project is its ability to produce project-standard or company-standard source code.

Coding standards are typically enforced through code reviews. The main function of a code review is to detect defects, but a secondary function is to bring all source code into alignment with the project's coding standards.

When the organization has a separate maintenance organization, it is useful to include someone from that organization in code reviews because that person will have a strong interest in seeing that the code is easy to maintain.

PROJECT OBJECTIVES

As they did during detailed design, developers should continue looking for ways to optimize the project goals during construction. Construction presents many opportunities to make the project simpler or more complex, more robust or more fragile, more nimble or more ponderous.

Developers will make literally thousands of low-level decisions about these factors during construction. This is no exaggeration. A medium-size program of 75,000 lines of code will be organized into perhaps 3,500 subroutines. Developers will make, on average, several decisions *per routine* that affect the software's complexity, robustness, and performance. They will decide how to document the routine, what coding style to use, how to handle errors, how to verify that the routine operates correctly, and, of course, how the routine actually performs its job. A clear project vision helps to ensure that many of these thousands of decisions are consistent with the project objectives. Lack of vision ensures that most of these decisions will be made without any particular focus.

———◆———

Software construction work is done at a very detailed level, and retrofitting these thousands of decisions would be tantamount to reimplementing the whole system. As a practical matter, if decisions are not made correctly the first time, you won't get a second chance.

———◆———

SIMPLICITY

Construction presents continuing opportunities for developers to simplify the program and make it less complex. Few projects are canceled because their designs and implementation weren't complicated enough. Many are canceled because they become so complicated that no one can understand them anymore; any attempt to change or extend the system results in so many unintended side effects that continuing to extend the system becomes practically impossible.

SOFTWARE INTEGRATION PROCEDURE

An important contributor to successful software construction is a Software Integration Procedure, which is the plan for integrating newly developed code into the main build. Table 14-1 shows the integration procedure I recommend.

TABLE 14-1   **RECOMMENDED INTEGRATION PROCEDURE**

1. Developer develops a piece of code.
2. Developer unit tests the code.
3. Developer steps through every line of code, including all exception and error cases, in an interactive debugger.
4. Developer integrates this preliminary code with a private version of the main build.
5. Developer submits code for technical review.
6. Developer informally turns code over to testing for test case preparation.
7. Code is reviewed.
8. Developer fixes any problems identified during the review.
9. Fixes are reviewed.
10. Developer integrates final code with the main build.
11. Code is declared "complete."

DONE IS DONE

The recommended integration procedure in Table 14-1 provides important project control benefits. It assures that when a piece of code is reported as "done," it really and truly is done. When you read a status report that says that "90 percent of modules are complete," you can have confidence that those modules really are complete and don't still contain a lot of hidden work.

Developers who are used to working with partial implementations will have to change their work habits to use this approach. Those developers are used to working on one part of the program and then discovering that their part of the program depends on functionality in another part of the program that isn't available yet. They'll detour to implement a quick-and-dirty version of the functionality they depend on, and then return to implementing the part they started with. Often the quick-and-dirty implementation contains limitations, and developers have to include workarounds in their main code to get around those limitations. The careful developers make notes to go back later and clean up the quick-and-dirty implementation. They then revise the main code to eliminate the workaround that was needed to use the quick-and-dirty routine.

Because this pattern of creating workarounds and then revising main code occurs many times over the course of a project, developers end up with enormous "to do" lists of items that say, "Go back and fix those quick-and-dirty parts I implemented and revise the parts of the main code that work around the limitations of the quick-and-dirty parts." This development approach implements a lot of visible functionality in a hurry, but it sets up the project for an open-ended clean-up phase in which the amount of work remaining is practically impossible to predict.

Using the integration procedure outlined in Table 14-1 requires discipline and is a significant adjustment for developers who have learned to base their development strategy on partial implementations. But the risk reduction, visibility, and control benefits of finishing each module completely before moving on to the next module make the practice worthwhile. This integration procedure will initially seem cumbersome to developers who haven't used it before, but the most serious inefficiencies on a software project arise from not detecting defects close to the time they are created. The recommended integration procedure prevents the vast majority of those defects from slipping through.

ENSURING A STABLE FOUNDATION FOR OTHER DEVELOPERS' WORK

This integration procedure also addresses the critical risk of problems in quality not becoming visible until late in the project. On poorly controlled projects, source code is integrated into the main project before its quality has been established. If no defects are immediately apparent, the developer forgets about the code and moves on to the next piece of work. Toward the end of the project, enough low quality code has been integrated that problems begin to surface, and, because each individual piece of code has not been required to meet high quality standards, fixing one problem typically creates two or three additional problems. At this point the project enters a mode that Microsoft calls "infinite defects"—defects are being created faster than they can be fixed, a trend which, if not altered, really would produce software with infinite defects. This risk of latent quality problems has caused the cancellation of hundreds if not thousands of projects; in response, the Software Integration Procedure is one way in which successful organizations eagerly trade a small increase in project overhead for a large reduction in project risk.

DAILY BUILD AND SMOKE TEST

A practice complementary to the Software Integration Procedure is the use of a daily build and smoke test, which is outlined in Table 14-2.

TABLE 14-2   DAILY BUILD AND SMOKE TEST PROCEDURE*

1. *Merge code changes.* The developer compares his or her private copy of the source files with the master source files, checking for conflicts and inconsistencies between recent changes made by other developers and the new or revised code to be added. The developer then merges his or her code changes with the master source files. The merging of code is usually supported by automated source code control tools, which warn the developer of any inconsistencies.

2. *Build and test a private release.* The developer builds and tests a private release to ensure that the newly implemented feature still works as expected.

3. *Execute the smoke test.* The developer runs the current smoke test against the private build to be sure the new code won't break the build.

4. *Check in.* The developer checks his or her private copies of the source code into the master source files. Some projects establish times during which new code can and can't be added to the daily build; for example, new code must be added no later than 5:00 p.m. and no earlier than 7:00 a.m.

5. *Generate the daily build.* The build team (or build person) generates a complete build of the software from the master sources.

6. *Run the smoke test.* The build team runs the smoke test to evaluate whether the build is stable enough to be tested.

7. *Fix any problems immediately!* If the build team discovers any errors that prevent the build from being tested (in other words, that break the build), it notifies the developer who checked the code that broke the build in, and that developer fixes the problem immediately. Fixing the build is the project's top priority.

---

*   The process in this table starts at Step 10 in Table 14-1's Recommended Integration Procedure, which is the point where the developer is ready to check in code. It assumes that the developer has checked out source code files that need to be changed and has possibly created new files.

In the daily build and smoke test process, the entire program is built every day. That means that every one of the program's source files is compiled, linked, and combined into an executable program every day. The software is then put through a "smoke test," a relatively simple test to see whether the software "smokes" or breaks when it's run. The term smoke test comes from electrical engineering, in which a test literally checks whether an electrical device smokes when it's turned on.

Every day, some effort will go into running the daily build and smoke test, tracking down developers responsible for breaking the build, and ensuring that those developers immediately fix the source code that broke the build. On small projects, the daily build can be performed by a quality assurance person in conjunction with that person's other responsibilities. On larger projects, a full-time person or even a group of people might be needed to conduct the daily build.

The smoke test should be updated throughout the project to keep pace with the developing software. Because it is run daily, the smoke test is often automated. The smoke test is not an exhaustive test, but it should cover enough of the software's functionality to support an evaluation of whether each day's build is stable enough to test. If the software isn't stable enough to test, the smoke test should fail the software.

The daily build and smoke test practice reduces the likelihood of one of the greatest risks that a team project faces: the risk that when the different team members combine or "integrate" the code they have been developing separately, the code doesn't work well together. This practice also addresses the risk of low quality. By at least minimally testing the full scope of the software every day, quality problems are prevented from taking control of the project. The project team brings the software to a known good state and then keeps it there. The software is simply not allowed to deteriorate to the point where time-consuming quality problems can occur.

Performing daily builds also makes it easier to monitor a project's progress. When the project team builds the system every day, the status of both complete and incomplete features is visible; both technical and nontechnical parties can simply exercise the software to get a sense of how close it is to completion.

This daily build and smoke test practice has been used successfully on projects of all sizes, including on the mammoth Microsoft Windows NT 3.0 project—a project with more than five million lines of code. The daily build and smoke test practice is especially important on large projects because the risk of unsuccessful integration is so significant.

Special Considerations for Stage 1

During Stage 1 construction, the development team should build a skeleton of the system that is sufficiently strong to support the rest of the system's functionality. Typically this involves creating a shell of the user interface that includes menus, a toolbar, and other places for attaching functionality as it is developed.

Building a skeleton of the system requires that some infrastructure be developed during Stage 1. Typically, low level tools such as error handlers, string handlers, and memory management will need to be constructed before much other implementation can take place. As Figure 14-1 suggests, in essence this calls for development of a roughly "T" shaped part of the system—the entire breadth of the system and a narrow vertical slice. This is referred to as a T shape because the whole breadth of the user interface is developed (but none of it works fully), and the entire depth of the supporting infrastructure is developed (but none of it is actually called yet by other functionality).

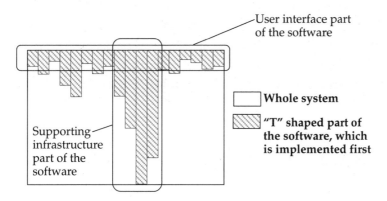

FIGURE 14-1   *Development of the system skeleton in a "T" shape during Stage 1 of the project. The entire breadth of the system is implemented as well as just enough depth to support the first stage's functionality.*

AVOIDING PREMATURE INFRASTRUCTURE DEVELOPMENT

As soon as the "T" is built, developing a fully functional slice of real, visible functionality is a good way to get the project moving quickly. Do *not* try to develop the full infrastructure before some amount of real functionality is delivered. (Infrastructure includes foundations, base classes, and other low-level code needed to support the program.)

In some theoretical sense, developing the complete infrastructure before implementing any visible functionality might be efficient, but in a practical sense, managers, customers, and developers begin to get nervous when too much time goes by before they can actually see the software work. Infrastructure development has the potential to become a research project in creating a perfect theoretical framework—a project that often ends up creating a lot of unnecessary functionality. The project team should implement only the part of the infrastructure needed to support the real functionality being delivered during the current stage. This approach works most efficiently because it brings the research project tendency to heel and flushes out problems in the infrastructure more quickly than abstract infrastructure development work does.

TRACKING PROGRESS

Tracking progress becomes a substantial job during construction. In earlier phases, the project work cannot be divided easily into small chunks, but during construction the work is divisible into miniature milestones, or tasks, that take a few days or less. In order to keep the project on track, the status of each of these tasks must be tracked.

COLLECTING STATUS INFORMATION

Automated tools substantially reduce the effort required to track miniature milestones. The list of miniature milestones should be contained in an electronic planning tool such as Microsoft Project or in a spreadsheet. This list should be stored in the project's revision control system and made accessible via the project's intranet home page, which will make it publicly available to the whole project team. When a developer or tester completes a milestone, he or she should check out the milestone list from revision control, update it to show that the task is complete, and check it back in.

The time-accounting system should be maintained similarly. Some organizations have project personnel fill out time sheets and then have administrative staff members perform the data entry. Once people become familiar with an automated system, however, doing the data entry online doesn't take any more time than filling out a time card. Project members should enter their time-accounting data into the time-accounting system at least weekly. When people enter their time-accounting data less often, they forget how they have really spent their time, and the accounting is inaccurate.

VISIBILITY

The streamlined collection of planning and time-accounting information is one way in which making planning materials publicly available is clearly beneficial to a project. It prevents the project manager from becoming the bottleneck for all status information. Another reason to keep materials in the project's public eye is that different project members will be sensitive to different issues. Together, visible project progress and an anonymous problem reporting and feedback channel go a long way toward ensuring that project management and upper management hear about emerging problems and have access to the information needed to address those problems.

WEEKLY PROJECT TRACKING UPDATE

About once a week during the construction phase, the project manager should review the project's status. This review should include several activities:

- Collecting summary data from the project planning, defect tracking, and time-accounting tools

- Comparing actual miniature milestones completed to the plan

- Comparing actual defects reported to predicted defects

- Comparing actual effort to planned effort

- Reviewing and updating the Top 10 Risks List

- Reviewing any feedback passed up through the anonymous feedback reporting channel

- Reviewing changes proposed and changes approved by the project change board, and reviewing the cumulative effect of those changes on the project plans

Based on this review, the project manager should take corrective action when the actual results and performance deviate significantly from the plans, or when emerging risks need to be addressed.

This weekly data collection and analysis also lays the foundation for updating the Software Project Log at the end of each stage and creating the Software Project History at the end of the project. (The Software Project Log is described in Chapter 17, "End-of-Stage Wrap-Up," and the Software Project History is described in Chapter 18, "Project History.")

COMMUNICATION WITH CUSTOMERS AND UPPER MANAGEMENT

As progress is reviewed, the project manager should be sure that it is communicated regularly to upper management, customers, users, and other project stakeholders so that they remain confident in the project. If the project manager waits for them to ask about the project, they are probably already nervous about it. At that point, the project manager can probably quiet their concerns but won't be able to regain their confidence.

The project manager should be proactive and tell project stakeholders how the project is going before they get nervous enough to ask. Most people would prefer to hear that "everything is okay" once a week rather than once a month. Managers and developers who have taken the initiative to keep project stakeholders regularly informed report far-reaching benefits such as being seen as more cooperative, responsive, and conscientious.

CONTROLLING CHANGES

As the software starts to become operational, users and managers will begin to use it (depending on the kind of software) and in the process discover that it deviates from what they were expecting. Some of these perceived deviations will occur because the software is a work in progress: is problem X a bug or is it something that isn't finished yet? Users and managers usually won't be able to tell just from using the software.

Some perceived deviations will really and truly call for changes in the software, and during construction, the pressure to change the software will pour in from all sources. If the project is otherwise under control at this point, uncontrolled changes will cause a project to blow its schedule and budget targets faster than any other factor.

———◆———

*The more the pressure to change the software
increases, the more important it becomes to address
changes deliberately, or the project
will slip out of control.*

———◆———

The project change board is the critical means of controlling changes. If the change board is to perform its function, the board's decisions must be respected by all project stakeholders, including upper managers, marketers, customers, and other people who typically initiate the most changes. Initiating the change board in the early days of the project, during requirements development, will give the board legitimacy by the time the project reaches construction. Everyone will be used to the process of submitting changes, notifying affected parties, considering all impacts, and then accepting the change board's decision.

People have a hard time integrating a systematic change control process into their work for the first time if they have to do it only three weeks before the software is supposed to be released. It's hard for them to respect the change board's authority if the board seems to have been set up for the express purpose of telling them "No." A long-standing change board prevents such a perception, and that *by itself* is a sufficient reason to set up the change board at the dawn of the project.

STAYING FOCUSED

Part of the project manager's job during this phase is to shield developers from distractions—especially requests for changes from users, upper management, marketers, and so on. The project manager should see that all change requests go through the official change control channels rather than straight to the developers so that the developers aren't distracted from their primary work.

Is That All There Is to Construction?

Construction is an activity of critical importance in software development. Good construction can make a project take half as long as bad construction. Good construction can lay the groundwork for generations of enjoyable software maintenance; bad construction can lay the groundwork for generations of agony and burgeoning expenses.

From a software project survival viewpoint, however, most of the groundwork for the project's ultimate success or failure has already been laid by the time the project reaches construction. If the team investigated requirements thoroughly, fleshed out its designs in detail, created a good architecture, mapped out a staged delivery plan, estimated the project carefully, and is controlling changes effectively, construction will be notable for its steady progress and *lack* of major problems.

———◆———

If upstream project stages have been conducted effectively, construction will be a time during which a great deal of work takes place uneventfully.

———◆———

Construction is the time when the tide begins to turn against poorly managed projects. Such projects appear to make rapid progress during early stages as they whiz through requirements development, architecture, and design with little effort, usually producing working code in short order. Problems become apparent only after enough code has been written for the software to be executed by testers and end users, who then begin to discover the software's many defects. At that point, problems can be corrected only at great cost. The poor practices that were initially disguised as rapid early progress are unmasked and found to be ill-conceived shortcuts. Development resources are invariably constrained, and the need to lengthen the schedule, increase the budget, and still leave many costly defects uncorrected gives rise to numerous painful confrontations between developers, testers, managers, and customers.

On well-run projects, these same problems are detected upstream when they can be corrected at much lower cost. The vast majority of problems detected during construction are construction problems, which can be corrected with little effort and without destructive confrontations.

212

Survival Check

 The project has a Coding Standard.

 The Coding Standard is enforced through technical reviews of all code.

 The project has a Software Integration Procedure.

 Developers aren't following the procedure.

 The project team builds a skeleton of the system during Stage 1.

 The project team gets bogged down building the complete infrastructure of the system before building any visible functionality.

 The project uses daily builds and smoke tests.

 The daily build is broken more often than not.

 The smoke test hasn't kept up with the daily build and doesn't test the software's full functionality.

 The project manager tracks relevant progress indicators weekly, including miniature milestones, defects, change reports, time-accounting data, and Top 10 Risks List.

 Project status data is readily available to all project members.

 Status isn't reported regularly to customers or upper management.

Changes are controlled through continuing use of the change control board.

The change control board wasn't set up until construction began, limiting its perceived authority.

15 *System Testing*

System testing is conducted in parallel with construction or a half step behind. It exercises the system from end to end, exposing defects that are then corrected by developers. Testers support developers by ensuring that the system's quality remains high enough to support the integration of new code. Developers support testers by correcting reported defects quickly.

System testing is performed to verify the end-to-end functionality of a system. It verifies that all requirements have been implemented and that they have been implemented at an acceptable quality level. On some projects, system testing is deferred to the end of the project. This chapter is logically distinct from the preceding chapter on software construction, but it is not chronologically distinct. System testing and construction activities should be happening at the same time.

Test Philosophy

Testing often becomes the critical-path activity on a software project because no one plans for it until the software is mostly complete. Without adequate preparation, ramping up test activities quickly enough to fully test the software is impossible, testing is inevitably abbreviated, and the software is released with many as-yet-to-be-detected defects.

In this book's approach, system tests are developed in lockstep with the software. Test cases should be implemented slightly ahead of or in conjunction with implementation of the software itself. On a project in which no one knows what the software will look like until it's actually developed, that testing strategy is impossible. But on projects that run according to this book's approach, testers will have a completely realistic User Interface Prototype and a detailed User Manual/Requirements Specification to employ in developing their test cases. Testers will also receive informal versions of the software at the same time the software is submitted for its code review. Test cases should be ready shortly after the software passes its code review.

Although in this book's approach system testing is developed right along with the software, the quality assurance role it plays is less dramatic than it is on projects that defer quality assurance until the end of the project. As Figure 15-1 illustrates, typical projects rely almost exclusively on testing to assure quality. Under this book's approach, by the time any particular functionality reaches system testing it will already have been reviewed during user-interface prototyping, User Manual/Requirements Specification review, architecture review, detailed design review, and code review. It will have been both unit tested and integration tested by its developer. And it will have passed the daily smoke test. That procedure simply doesn't leave many places for additional defects to hide, which is the reason that system testing becomes less prominent.

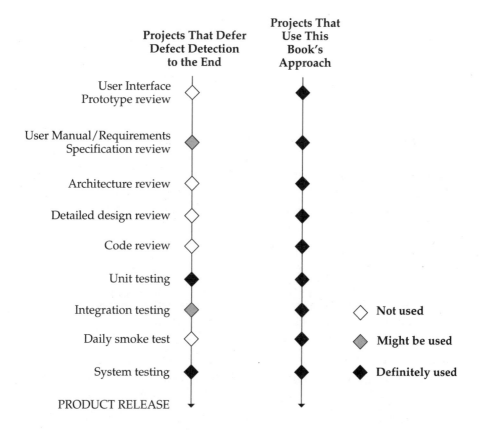

FIGURE 15-1   *Development of functionality using a typical approach compared with using this book's approach.*

EXTENT OF SYSTEM TESTING

System testing should test the entire scope of a system. Test cases should be designed to assure that each requirement is implemented and each line of code is executing without errors.

System testing during each stage of a staged delivery project should consist of adding new test cases to cover requirements implemented during the current stage and "regression testing" the requirements delivered in previous stages to be sure that new code hasn't broken old code.

TEST GROUP'S SUPPORT FOR DAILY BUILDS

Typically, the test group will perform a smoke test each day to verify that the daily build can be tested. The smoke test, which usually takes a half hour or less, determines whether the day's build is sufficiently stable to enter system testing. If the build fails the smoke test, the test group kicks it back to the development group for immediate correction.

Developer's Support for System Testing

Developers need to fix defects quickly so that the testing team doesn't twiddle its thumbs while waiting for a build that's stable enough to test. The weekly project-tracking materials should include a chart that lists the number of unresolved defects. This number should be kept small. You can keep the quality level of the software high by requiring developers to keep their unresolved defect counts below 10 (or some other number that makes sense for your project). This practice helps to rein in fast but sloppy programmers by not allowing them to work on new features when they are responsible for a lot of unresolved defects.

Developers will sometimes resist correcting defects as they are detected. They will typically argue that taking time to fix defects distracts them from the main work they are doing and makes them less efficient. *Do not accept this argument.* What they don't realize is that their buggy code is making both the testers' work and other developers' work less efficient. Other developers will waste time trying to figure out why code they have just written doesn't work and will eventually track the problem to a known defect in another programmer's code. Any way you look at it, time spent diagnosing a problem that has already been reported is time wasted. If that problem was reported only a few hours earlier, the time another developer spends rediagnosing the same problem can be written off as an unavoidable inefficiency. But if that defect was reported a few days earlier, the wasted time was totally avoidable—the problem should have been corrected promptly, before anyone had to waste time diagnosing it again.

Strategic Quality Assurance

System testing can be used not just to fix specific defects but to take strategic action to improve the quality of the software. Commonly, about 80 percent of a system's errors will be found in about 20 percent of its routines. Several software engineering studies have found that these routines contribute a disproportionate share of the total cost to a system.

Use the defect tracking system to identify the routines that are producing the majority of the system's errors. Any routine that has been responsible for more than 10 errors is a candidate. Conduct remedial design reviews of those routines to bring them up to standard. Selectively redesign and reimplement the most troublesome ones.

———◆———

On a typical project, about 80 percent of the time is spent on unplanned rework. Performing a small amount of strategic, planned rework can dramatically improve software quality and the project's overall productivity.

———◆———

Survival Check

 System testing is ready to go at the same time as construction.

 Testers smoke test the daily build and return the build to development if it fails.

 The build often fails the smoke test because developers are not unit testing their own code adequately.

 Developers don't fix defects quickly after they are reported.

 Testing identifies error-prone routines for developers to review and then redesign or reimplement.

16 *Software Release*

Driving the software to a releasable condition at the end of each stage is essential to managing the risks of unsuccessful integration and poor quality. Determining whether the software is good enough to release is difficult to do intuitively. Fortunately, several simple statistical techniques can help with that determination. The release stage can be a hectic time, and the use of a Release Checklist helps avoid problems.

As each stage winds to a close, the project team will either symbolically or literally release the software. Whether symbolic or literal, driving the software to a releasable state at the end of each stage is important. The defect count should be brought down to a point where the software could be released to the public, fit-and-finish issues should be addressed, the user documentation should be brought into alignment with the as-built software, and so on.

TREATING RELEASES SERIOUSLY

Overlapping the release phase of one stage with the detailed design phase of the next stage is often a good idea. On a project that doesn't use design and code reviews, developers are held hostage by defect corrections during the release stage. On a project that has done a good job of assuring quality throughout the stage, there won't be enough release-related work to keep developers busy full time, and they will be eager to move on to the next stage.

There are strong temptations to treat part-time release work as a secondary priority. Developers will be more eager to begin work in new areas than to fix problems in old areas. Making progress on new designs and implementations will seem more productive than fixing minor problems with old work.

—————◆—————

The entire project team should treat driving the software to a releasable state at the end of each stage as its top priority.

—————◆—————

The success of the staged delivery approach relies on bringing the software to a releasable quality level and embracing all the extra quality assurance and development work that that entails. Bringing the software to a releasable condition eliminates dark corners in which unforeseen work can accumulate, improving status visibility. If the release phase of a particular stage is allowed to drag on for weeks or months while most of the project team has moved on to the next stage, the ability to determine the project's true status will be lost.

Driving to a releasable state also eliminates the places where insidious quality problems can hide. Without periodically raising the software's quality to a releasable level, the software will begin a slow slide toward low quality, whence it may never return.

I audited a project on which the developers had originally planned to deliver the software in stages. As they approached the end of Stage 1, they decided that they didn't have time to drive the software to a releasable condition, so they moved directly into the development work for Stage 2. By the time my audit team reviewed that project's progress, the project was months behind schedule, mostly because the developers were stuck in an extended test-debug-correct-test cycle. Every defect they fixed seemed to give rise to at least one more defect.

The root of the project's problem was that it had accumulated a large mass of low quality code. When developers added new code, they couldn't tell whether new defects originated from the new code or from the low quality old code. That dramatically increased the time required to debug problems, and made their corrections more error prone. The team finally worked its way out of the situation by calling a complete halt to new code development and focusing the developers solely on fixing defects for more than a month.

The developers' decision at the end of Stage 1 that they "didn't have time" to drive the software to a releasable state was one of the most costly decisions they could have made. They probably were behind schedule when they made that decision. But their decision ultimately put them further behind schedule. If they had stuck to their original plan and had driven their software to a releasable condition at the end of Stage 1, they would have reduced their subsequent test, debug, and correction efforts by a huge factor.

Developers can begin working on the detailed design for the next stage during the release phase of the current stage, but they must be ready to drop their design work at a moment's notice to correct defects detected in the previous stage's work.

WHEN TO RELEASE

The question of whether to release software is a treacherous one. The answer must teeter on the line between releasing poor quality software early and releasing high quality software late. The questions of "Is the software good enough to release now?" and "When will the software be good enough to release?" can become critical to a company's survival. Several techniques can help you base the answers to these questions on a firmer footing than can the instinctive guesses that are sometimes used.

DEFECT COUNTS

At the most basic level, defect counts give you a quantitative handle on how much work the project team has to do before it can release the software. You can get a summary of the number of remaining defects remaining in order of priority: "2 critical defects, 8 serious defects, 147 cosmetic defects," and so on.

By comparing the number of new defects to the number of defects resolved each week, you can determine how close the project is to completion. If the number of new defects in a particular week exceeds the number of defects resolved that week, the project still has miles to go. Figure 16-1 shows an "open defects" graph, which tracks the status of defects.

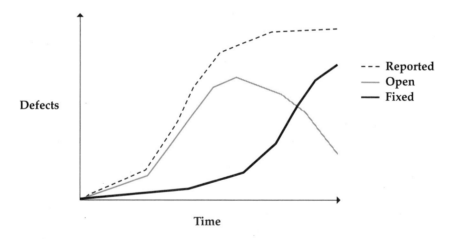

FIGURE 16-1   *Example of an "open defects" graph. Making this graph public emphasizes that controlling defects is a high priority and helps to keep potential quality problems under control.*

If the project's quality level is under control and the project is making progress toward completion, the number of open defects should generally trend downward after the middle of the project and then remain low. The point at which the "fixed" defects line crosses the "open" defects line is psychologically significant because it indicates that defects are being corrected faster than they are being found. If the project's quality level is out of control and the project is thrashing (not making any real progress toward completion), you might see a steadily increasing number of open defects. This suggests that steps need to be taken to improve the quality of the existing designs and code before adding more new functionality.

STATISTICS ON EFFORT PER DEFECT

The data on time required to fix defects categorized by type of defect will provide a basis for estimating remaining defect-correction work on this and future projects. When you collect this information, by the middle of the project you'll be able to say things like, "The project has 230 open defects, and the developers have been averaging 3 hours per defect correction, so the project has approximately 700 hours of defect correction activity remaining."

The data on phases in which defects are detected and corrected also gives you a measure of the efficiency of the development process. If 95 percent of the defects are detected in the same phase they were created, the project has a very efficient process. If 95 percent of the defects are detected one or more phases after the phase in which they were created, the project has a lot of room for improvement.

DEFECT DENSITY PREDICTION

One of the easiest ways to judge whether a program is ready to release is to measure its defect density—the number of defects per line of code. Suppose that the first version of your software, GigaTron 1.0, consisted of 100,000 lines of code, that the quality assurance group detected 650 defects prior to the software's release, and that another 50 defects were reported after the software was released. The software therefore had a lifetime defect count of 700 defects, and a defect density of 7 defects per thousand lines of code (KLOC).

Suppose that GigaTron 2.0 consisted of 50,000 additional lines of code, that QA detected 400 defects prior to release, and another 75 after release. The total defect density of that release would be 475 total defects divided by 50,000 new lines of code, or 9.5 defects per KLOC.

Now suppose that you're trying to decide whether the GigaTron 3.0 has been tested enough to release. It consists of 100,000 new lines of code, and QA has detected 600 defects so far, or 6 defects per KLOC. Unless you have a good reason to think that the development team's development process has improved with this project, your experience should lead you to expect between 7 and 10 defects per KLOC. The number of defects the project team should attempt to find will vary depending on the level of quality you're aiming for. If you want to remove 95 percent of all defects before releasing the software, the project team would need to detect somewhere between 650 and 950 prerelease defects. This technique suggests that the software is not quite ready to release.

The more historical project data you have, the more confident you can be in the prerelease defect density targets. If you have data from only two projects and the range is as broad as 7 to 10 defects per KLOC, that leaves a lot of wiggle room for an expert judgment about whether the third project will be more like the first or the second. But if you've tracked defect data for 10 projects and found that their average lifetime defect rate is 7.4 defects per KLOC with a standard deviation of 0.4 defects, you have a great deal of guidance indeed.

Defect Pooling

Another simple defect prediction technique is to separate defect reports into two pools. Call them Pool A and Pool B. The testing team then tracks the defects in these two pools separately. The distinction between the two pools is essentially arbitrary. You could split the testing team down the middle and put half of its reported defects into one pool, half into the other. It doesn't really matter how you make the division as long as both reporting pools operate independently and both test the full scope of the software.

Once you create a distinction between the two pools, the testing team tracks the number of defects reported in Pool A, the number in Pool B—and here's the important part—the number of defects that are reported in both Pool A and Pool B. The number of unique defects reported at any given time is this:

$$Defects_{Unique} = Defects_A + Defects_B - Defects_{A\&B}$$

The number of total defects can then be estimated by using this simple formula:

$$Defects_{Total} = (Defects_A * Defects_B) / Defects_{A\&B}$$

If the GigaTron 3.0 project has 400 defects in Pool A, 350 defects in Pool B, and 150 of the defects in both pools, as is shown in Figure 16-2, the number of unique defects detected would be $400 + 350 - 150 = 600$. The approximate number of total defects would be $(400 * 350) / 150 = 933$. This technique suggests that there are approximately 333 defects yet to be detected (about a third of the estimated total defects). Use of this technique reveals that quality assurance on this example project still has a long way to go.

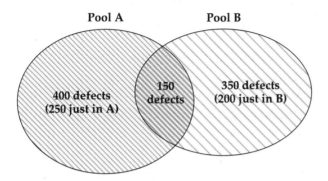

FIGURE 16-2   *Defect pooling. The number of unique defects can be estimated based on the overlap of defects reported in the separate pools.*

The defect pooling technique involves a significant amount of overhead in keeping track of two separate lists of defects and identifying the defects that are common to both lists. It also involves the overhead of covering the entire scope of the software with two independent testing groups. Because of the overhead involved, this technique is best suited to projects that need to be especially accurate in determining their remaining defects prior to release.

DEFECT SEEDING

As Figure 16-3 on the next page suggests, defect seeding is inspired by a well-developed statistical technique in which a sample from a population is extracted and used to estimate the total population. For example, to estimate the number of fish in a pond, biologists would tag a certain number of fish and release them back into the pond. They would then capture a sample of fish and compare the number of tagged and untagged fish that were captured to estimate the total number of fish in the pond.

Defect seeding is a practice in which defects are intentionally inserted into a program by one group for detection by another group. The ratio of the number of seeded defects detected to the total number of defects seeded provides a rough idea of the total number of program defects that have been detected.

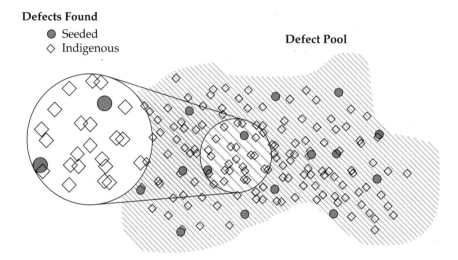

Defects Found
- ● Seeded
- ◇ Indigenous

Defect Pool

FIGURE 16-3   *Defect seeding. Defects can be estimated based on the ratio of seeded defects found to indigenous defects found.*

Suppose that on GigaTron 3.0, the development team intentionally seeded the program with 50 errors. For best effect, the team's seeded errors should be designed to cover the full breadth of the software's functionality, and they should also cover the full range of severities—from crashing errors to cosmetic errors.

Suppose that at a point in the project when you believe testing to be almost complete, you look at the seeded defect report. You find that 31 seeded defects and 600 indigenous defects have been reported. You can estimate the total number of defects with this formula:

$$Defects_{Total} = (Defects_{SeededDefectsPlanted} / Defects_{SeededDefectsFound}) * Defects_{FoundSoFar}$$

According to this formula, GigaTron 3.0 has approximately this number of total defects: (50 / 31) * 600 = 968. Almost 400 defects have yet to be detected.

To use defect seeding, the developers must seed the defects prior to the beginning of the tests whose effectiveness you want to ascertain. If the testing team uses manual methods and has no systematic way of covering the same testing ground twice, the developers should seed defects before that testing begins. If the testing team uses fully automated regression tests, the developers can seed defects virtually any time to ascertain the number of indigenous defects the automated tests have detected.

A common problem with defect seeding programs is forgetting to remove the seeded defects. Another common problem is that removing poorly designed seeded defects can introduce new errors. To prevent these problems, be sure to remove all seeded defects prior to final system testing and software release. Some projects require that seeded defects be kept extremely simple, and they allow introduction of only those seeded defects that can be created by adding exactly one line of code.

DEFECT MODELING

With software defects, no news is usually bad news. If the project has reached a late stage with few defects reported, there is a natural tendency to think, "We finally got it right and created a program with almost no defects!" In reality, no news is more often the result of insufficient testing than of superlative development practices.

Some of the more sophisticated software project estimation and control tools[1] contain defect modeling functionality that can predict the number of defects you should expect to find at each stage of a project . By comparing the number of defects actually detected to the number predicted, you can assess whether the project is keeping up with defect detection or lagging behind.

THE RELEASE DECISION

If you follow the practices described in this book, you'll have solid information upon which to base the decision about whether software is ready to release. These sources of information include the following:

- Code growth statistics and graph (refer to Figure 5-6 on page 62)
- Detailed list of binary miniature milestones completed
- List of raw defects from the defect tracking system
- Cumulative defect statistics and graph (refer to Figure 16-1 on page 224)

---

1. For a current list of these tools, see the *Survival Guide* Web site.

- Effort-per-defect statistics
- Defect density prediction
- Defect pooling
- Defect seeding
- Defect modeling

Evaluating combinations of these readiness indicators will give you more confidence than you could have from evaluating any of the techniques individually. Examining defect density alone on GigaTron 3.0 suggested that you should expect 700 to 1000 total lifetime defects, and the project team should remove 650 to 950 defects before software release to achieve 95 percent prerelease defect removal. If the project team had detected 600 defects, the defect density information alone might have led you to declare the software "almost ready to release." But defect pooling analysis estimated that GigaTron 3.0 will produce approximately 933 total defects. Comparing the results of those two techniques suggests that you should expect a total defect count toward the high end of the defect density range instead of the low end. Because the defect seeding technique also estimated a total number of defects in the 900s, it seems evident that GigaTron 3.0 will exhibit a relatively large total number of defects and that the project should continue testing.

DEFECT TRACKING AND COMMUNICATION

Publicizing the kind of status and quality information discussed in this section helps to keep the project on track. The project team should post defect summary information in a public place, such as in the project break room, on the project manager's office door, or on a project intranet Web page.

RELEASE CHECKLIST

At the end of a stage, even on the best projects, the most serious errors committed are often simple oversights. People want their work to be done, feel that it is done, and have a tendency to skip seemingly obvious details.

Very early in my software career I was the project manager for an insurance consulting company that provided insurance rate quotation programs for its clients. These were very simple programs by today's standards, each involving no more than about 3 staff-months of effort to create, and most requiring considerably less development time. Even with these simple programs, we managed to run into the most common problem with software releases—simply forgetting some of the things we knew we needed to do before we released the software to our clients! As a result of our hard-won experience, we created a Release Checklist, which included items like this:

◆   Make exact duplicates of diskettes before sending them out.

◆   Make a list of all the people receiving the program and the number of diskettes mailed to them.

◆   Put postage on packages sent to clients.

If you read between the lines, you might guess that at one time we didn't keep exact copies of the programs we mailed out and couldn't reproduce problems clients reported. We sometimes didn't know which clients had received which programs, and one time we even forgot to include postage on a program we sent to a client.

More sophisticated applications require more sophisticated release procedures, but the basis of any release procedure will still be a checklist of activities that need to be done before the software can be released, and that checklist will inevitably consist of many activities that were forgotten at one time or another. A Release Checklist for a simple program might contain only a handful of items. The Release Checklist for an extremely complicated program such as Microsoft Windows 95 might contain 200 items or more.

Table 16-1 (on pages 232–233) shows some of the items that should be included on the Release Checklist for a medium-sized software product that will be released to the general public. The focus of the list is not on testing— by this time it is too late in the project to start worrying about that. The focus is on items that are easily overlooked in the haste to push the software out the door.

If the project team is releasing the software to in-house users, the checklist will look different, but the same idea applies: the checklist should capture the critical release activities the project team doesn't want to forget in the rush to release the new system. The project team should put together Release Checklists for interim releases and for the final release. The different lists will not be identical but will have many points in common.

TABLE 16-1   **SAMPLE ITEMS ON THE RELEASE CHECKLIST**

Activities	Person Responsible
Engineering Activities	
☐ Update version strings with final version information.	Developer
☐ Remove debugging and testing code from the software.	Developer
☐ Remove seeded defects from the software.	Developer
Quality Assurance Activities	
☐ Check that all defects on current defect list have been resolved.	Tester
☐ Smoke test/regression test final build.	Tester
☐ Install program from CD ROM on clean machine.	Tester
☐ Install program from diskettes on clean machine.	Tester
☐ Install program from Internet Web site on clean machine.	Tester
☐ Install program from CD ROM/diskettes on machine with older version of program (upgrade install).	Tester
☐ Verify that the correct Windows registry entries have been created by the install program (see attached list).	Tester
☐ Verify uninstall on clean machine.	Tester
Release Activities	
☐ Freeze final list of files to be distributed.	Release team
☐ Synchronize date/time stamp on all release files.	Release team
☐ Prepare final program disks ("gold disks").	Release team

(continued)

TABLE 16-1   **SAMPLE ITEMS ON THE RELEASE CHECKLIST** *continued*

Activities	Person Responsible
☐ Verify that all files are present on the gold disks.	Release team
☐ Virus scan all release media.	Release team
☐ Surface scan the master media for bad sectors.	Release team
☐ Create a backup of the build environment and place the development environment under change control.	Release team
Documentation Activities	
☐ Verify version of readme.txt on gold disks.	Documentation team
☐ Verify version of help files on gold disks.	Documentation team
Other Activities	
☐ Verify copyright, license, and other legal materials.	Product manager, legal advisor

RELEASE SIGN-OFF FORM

In addition to the Release Checklist, most organizations have the release signed off by all concerned parties. If the project team is releasing software to the general public, it's important that it have a check in place to prevent bad software from being rushed into the public's hands. Leading edge organizations require software to be approved by quality assurance before it can be released. Quality assurance is sometimes treated as a second-class activity by project leaders whose backgrounds are on the development side, but quality assurance is what prevents the team from releasing software that is embarrassing, becomes a costly technical support burden, or, in the worst case, exposes the organization to legal liabilities. I advise requiring the approval of quality assurance before software is released and not pressuring quality assurance to approve the release until it is confident that the software is adequate.

Some people worry that quality assurance zealots will hold the software hostage until every last bug has been corrected, and this is where the measurable release criteria I described in Chapter 9 come in handy. When the project has measurable release criteria—such as "95 percent of all Sev 1 and Sev 2 defects corrected"—quality assurance's job is simply to report whether the software satisfies the release criteria that everyone agreed to months earlier.

In addition to the quality assurance group, other stakeholders often need to approve release of new software. A representative list of stakeholders is shown in Table 16-2.

TABLE 16-2 **SAMPLE RELEASE SIGN-OFF FORM**

Identification

Program Name _____

Program Version _____

Project Code Name _____

Sign-Offs

I certify that this software is ready to be released:

Engineering Lead for Subsystem 1 _____

Engineering Lead for Subsystem 2 _____

... ...

Engineering Lead for Subsystem n _____

Engineering Manager _____

Product Manager _____

Quality Assurance Manager _____

Documentation Manager _____

International Engineering Manager _____

User Support Manager _____

Marketing Manager _____

Legal _____

Using a Release Checklist and a Release Sign-Off Form cannot guarantee a perfect release, but not using them almost guarantees a faulty one. Release Checklists are easy to use, easy to keep up to date, and can make the difference between a strong release and one that ends up marked "return to sender."

Survival Check

 The project team treats the end-of-stage release phase as its top priority.

 Statistical techniques are used to aid the release decision.

 Only one statistical technique is used.

 The project team uses a Release Checklist to prevent oversights during software release.

 The project team uses the Release Sign-Off Form to ensure that all project stakeholders agree the software is ready to release.

17 End-of-Stage Wrap-Up

The end of a stage provides an opportunity to make course corrections and learn from the experience of the stage. Increasingly accurate estimates can be made as the project progresses, laying the groundwork for planning that will be done at the beginning of the next stage. Project experience to date should be recorded in a Software Project Log so that it can be used by future projects.

S taged delivery is a flexible delivery approach, and a Staged Delivery Plan can be executed with either of two general bents:

◆ The stages can be deterministic, which means that they mainly provide a means of delivering the most important software functionality earlier than would be possible with an all-at-once approach.

◆ The content of the stages can be redefined at the end of each stage, which means that the stages deliver the most important functionality early but also provide an opportunity to change course at the end of each stage.

In either approach, the end of each stage presents an opportunity to learn from the experience gained during the stage and to apply it to the next stage. Staged delivery enables the project team to gain experience and expertise more rapidly than do approaches in which the team delivers the software only once per project.

HOLD AN OMNIBUS CHANGE BOARD MEETING

The time just after a release is a natural time to consider proposed feature changes en masse. The whole project team typically works hard to achieve its software release, and spending a day or two considering proposed changes can provide a welcome change of pace. Hold an omnibus change board meeting at which changes deferred during the stage are evaluated. Project members (other than the change board members) shouldn't be subjected to a continuous barrage of feature change requests. If the number of times changes are considered is not limited, project members can find themselves evaluating change impacts every few days or so, and those little bits of work add up to a huge distraction. Defect corrections are a special kind of change—defects can and should be corrected continuously throughout the stage.

Deferring feature change evaluations until the end of the stage also provides better prioritization of changes because change proposals are grouped together. If the change board evaluates changes every week, it can approve some insignificant changes just because no other changes were proposed that week, and approving an extra half day's work doesn't seem as though it will do any harm. Over the course of a project, however, those half days can add up to major schedule slips, especially if the estimated half days turn out to be actual full days.

RECALIBRATE ESTIMATES

The end of a stage is a good time to review the project's actual schedule performance against its planned schedule performance and revise the project estimates. Reexamine the various factors that went into creating the estimate in the first place by considering these questions:

◆   Is the project scope still about the same as it was estimated to be originally? If not, the estimate should be adjusted for the improved understanding of the project scope.

◆   Has the feature set been changed?

◆   Has the required level of performance, robustness, or fit and finish changed?

◆   Has the development team been as productive as expected?

◆   Were necessary tasks omitted from the estimates? The estimates should be revised to account for these factors, too.

———◆———

It isn't wrong to underestimate the project's size or overestimate the project team's productivity early in the project; it's wrong not to find and correct those estimation mistakes later in the project.

———◆———

REESTIMATING PRODUCTIVITY

Suppose the project plan originally called for the project to be completed in six months and for the first stage to be delivered in eight weeks. Suppose the first stage actually took 10 weeks. How should the development team recalibrate its estimates for the rest of the project? Here are a few typical approaches:

◆   Assume it can make up the lost two weeks later in the schedule, and keep the 6-month total estimate.

◆   Add two weeks to the total schedule, creating a 6.5-month schedule.

◆   Multiply the whole schedule by the magnitude of the slip, in this case by 25 percent, for a 7.5-month schedule.

The first approach in the preceding list is the most common. A few tasks are usually overlooked in the original estimates, which accounts for some of the extra time used, and project members will vow that no similar oversights lurk in the other estimates. People typically convince themselves that the first part of the project took longer than expected because there was more to learn during that phase than they expected. They convince themselves that they have learned so much during this phase that the next phases can't help but go faster.

Do not fall victim to this reasoning! Software development is inherently an exercise in climbing steep learning curves—an exercise in problem solving—and the learning curves don't disappear at the end of the first stage.

———◆———

*A 1991 survey of over 300 projects found that
projects hardly ever make up lost time—
they tend to get further behind.*

———◆———

The second approach might seem more reasonable, but estimates of this type tend to be inaccurate for systemic reasons that pervade the whole schedule. For example, the project team feels pressure to use optimistic assumptions, or the team rushes through project estimation and thus overlooks many small but necessary activities in the estimates. The software organization's actual experience is likely to be more accurate than estimates made early in the project. The project team can look for root causes (other than mistaken productivity assumptions) for the missed deadline, but within a single project, root causes tend to be hard to correct.

With rare exception, the most accurate way to recalibrate a schedule is the third approach: multiplying the whole schedule by the magnitude of the slip. That approach weights the project's real experience more heavily than estimates made early in the project and is based on actual rather than planned performance.

"Reestimate" or "Slip"?

In some organizations, a reestimate will be perceived as a "slip" rather than as the inevitable refinement that occurs as a development team gains an increasingly detailed understanding of the software they are building.

The terms "reestimate" and "slip" have different connotations. A reestimate is a calculated, planned event based on the understanding that creating pinpoint-accurate software project estimates early in a project is theoretically impossible. Reestimates take place at points in the project that are predefined in the project plan. Periodic reestimation is a sign of a competent development team.

A slip is a failure to meet a milestone. It is a sign that management has not sufficiently motivated the development team, or that the development team is not sufficiently skilled to meet its commitments. Slips occur unpredictably, typically in conjunction with missing a major milestone.

———◆———

If the project stakeholders don't understand the reestimation plan from the beginning of the project, the development team's reestimates will be perceived as slips.

———◆———

Be sure that all project stakeholders understand from day one that, on a healthy, successful project, development teams refine their estimates at predetermined moments over the course of the project.

Evaluate Performance Against the Project Plan

How well did the team perform compared with the project plan? Did the project team follow the procedures required by the project plan throughout the stage? Did it perform technical reviews, follow the integration procedure, observe the Change Control Plan, keep track of time-accounting data, and follow the plan in other respects? If not, why not? Was the plan impossible to follow, or was the team simply not diligent about the way it performed during the stage?

---◆---

One of the most common software project
management problems is abandoning the project
plan without any real intention to do so.

---◆---

Development teams abandon their plans for many reasons. With this book's approach, the plans are more likely to be followed, for several reasons:

◆   The plans are publicly available. On some projects, teams don't follow the plans because they can't find them!

◆   The plans are credible. The development team participated in the creation of the plans and should believe they're realistic and can be followed.

◆   The plans are humane. The plans represent a sincere attempt to map a course for the project with only a small amount of surgical overtime. They aren't a ruse to goad the team into working unpaid overtime.

◆   The plans are kept up-to-date. The plans don't get so far out of touch with the project reality that they become impossible to follow.

Stick to the plan. If the plan is impossible to follow, replan. A sure way to lose control of the project is to abandon the original plan without putting a new plan in its place.

ARCHIVE PROJECT MEDIA

At the end of each stage, the entire environment used to create the software should be archived. Organizations often need to be able to recreate an old version of their software, which can be an impossible task if old versions of project components are unavailable. The project should archive at least the following materials:

◆   Copies of the release package, including CDs or diskettes, printed user documentation, collateral material, and packaging

◆   Source code

◆   Database or data files released with the software

◆   Data files used to create the software

◆   Custom tools developed for use on the project

- Commercial libraries

- Graphic resources, video resources, sound resources, and other resources contained in the software

- Compiler, linker, resource compiler, and other tools used to create the software

- Source text files for help files and other documentation

- Build scripts

- Test scripts

- Test data

One copy of each of these materials should be stored with the project archives, and another copy should be stored at a safe offsite facility. Working documents, spreadsheets, project plans, and other materials that have been placed under change control should also be archived along with versions of the word processor, spreadsheet program, project planning software, and other tools used to create them.

End-of-stage archiving is a not a substitute for periodic backups. If you're in the business of developing software, not backing up regularly is like running a convenience store and leaving your cash lying on the counter. The results of your hard work are too vulnerable to both accidental and intentional loss.

UPDATE THE SOFTWARE PROJECT LOG

Effective organizations collect information about projects as they are running so that what they learn can be made available to help future projects. Collecting this information at the end of each stage throughout the project allows someone looking back at the project to get a dynamic picture of its progress in addition to its final schedule and budget tally.

Project records are kept in a Software Project Log, which the project manager should update to describe the project's status at the end of each stage. Table 17-1 on the following page shows an outline of the contents of a Software Project Log.

Once the material listed in Table 17-1 has been collected and the Software Project Log has been updated, the log should be updated in the change control system. This document, like all other project planning documents, should be made publicly available throughout the project.

TABLE 17-1   **CONTENTS OF THE SOFTWARE PROJECT LOG**

Current project estimates for schedule and effort

Adjustments to schedule and effort approved by the change board during the stage

Dates, background, and results of major decisions during the stage

Planned vs. actual dates for each of the stage's major deliverables

Results of technical reviews conducted during the stage (pass/fail status and defect statistics)

Time-accounting data

Lines of code

Defect count

Number of changes proposed and accepted

Updating the Software Project Log requires amazingly little time (an hour or two if all the project tracking materials are up-to-date) and pays back huge benefits in the foundation it lays for future project planning—including future stages of the current project.

Survival Check

 The project team defers feature change requests until the end of each stage.

 The project team also defers defect corrections until the end of each stage.

 The project team reestimates effort, schedule, and cost at the end of each stage.

 Reestimation assumes the estimation error will be added to end of schedule rather than multiplied across the entire schedule.

 Reestimation is perceived as a slip instead of an estimate because stakeholders weren't educated about reestimation at the beginning of the project.

 The project manager records project status in the Software Project Log at the end of each stage.

IV

MISSION ACCOMPLISHED

18 *Project History*

Information stored in a project's Software Project History document will be useful to future projects. The Software Project History uses data from the Software Project Log, which is updated at the end of each stage; the project history distills general lessons from that data. On well-run projects, most of the data needed for the Software Project History will be readily available and the project history will be easy to create.

D epending on the length and scope of the project, the postrelease period is a time to treat the project team to a nice dinner, give them the afternoon off, or send them to Hawaii for a well-deserved vacation. Whether the project has been a stomping success or a foot-dragging failure, it is also a time to learn from the experience and build a foundation for future successes.

Gathering Project Data

Some projects hold a project review (postmortem) meeting at the end of the project. Others collect e-mail summaries of what each project member thinks has worked and not worked. Regardless of the specific data-gathering technique, gathering the project members' subjective impressions about what worked and what did not is important and gathering that information soon after the project is completed is a good idea.

For best results, collect the project members' impressions about the project within 15 to 30 days of releasing the software. After more time than that, project members begin to forget important insights, and assembling or reconstructing end-of-project status data becomes more difficult.

Project Review Meeting

Project review meetings can be valuable times for project members to discuss their insights candidly, and those insights can be tremendously beneficial to the organization. When the project team holds a project review meeting, it should be sure to use an objective moderator because project review meetings can degenerate into gripe sessions. The gripes will be fresh, and project members will want to discuss them. An objective moderator will make sure that all sides of each major issue are discussed and will keep the members from getting mired in any single topic.

Some projects have had good experience using a three-part project review questionnaire. The first part contains numerical rankings of various project attributes: "How would you rate the project's control over changing requirements on a scale of one to five with one being too restrictive, five being too lax, and three being just right?" This allows project members' subjective evaluations of the project to be compiled in a quasi-quantitative form.

The second part contains targeted questions about specific areas that might need improvement. This part might include specific questions, such as "We used a staged delivery approach for the first time on this project. In your opinion, how helpful was that in meeting our project's objectives? How could the approach be improved?" The questions in this part can be used to direct discussion during the project review meeting. The third part is a free-form comments area, which can be used to solicit open-ended comments.

In addition to the structure it provides, this kind of questionnaire can be used to solicit anonymous feedback, which in some environments might be more candid than face-to-face feedback.

SOFTWARE PROJECT HISTORY DOCUMENT

As mentioned earlier, the project history is formalized in a document called a Software Project History. A good Software Project History collects both objective, quantitative information about what happened on the project and the team members' subjective, qualitative impressions of what worked well and what didn't.

The combination of quantitative information from the Software Project Log and subjective insights from the project review will make up the Software Project History, which is outlined in Table 18-1 on the following page.

TABLE 18-1   **CONTENTS OF THE SOFTWARE PROJECT HISTORY**

Introduction

Describe the software's purpose, customer, vision statement, detailed objectives, and other general information.

Historical Overview

For each phase, describe the work products produced, milestones, major risks addressed, schedules, staffing levels, and other project planning information.

Describe the following phases:

User-interface prototyping and requirements gathering

Architectural design

Quality assurance planning

General stage planning

Activities from detailed design through release (including detailed design, construction, system testing, and stage releases) for each stage $1 - n$

Final software release

Project Data

Describe the organizational structure used, including the executive sponsor, project participants, their roles, and their levels of participation over the course of the project.

The Software Project History should also contain the following hard data about the project:

Actual schedule and effort as of the release date

Time-accounting data as of the release date

Number of subsystems as of the release date

Lines of source code as of the release date

Lines of reused code as of the release date

Amount of media (sound, graphics, video, and so on)

Defect count as of the release date

Number of changes proposed and accepted as of the release date

Graph showing each schedule estimate compared to the actual schedule over time

Graph showing each effort estimate compared to the actual effort over time

Graph of project's code growth by week

Graph of project's open and closed defect count by week

(continued)

TABLE 18-1   CONTENTS OF THE SOFTWARE PROJECT HISTORY *continued*

Lessons Learned

Describe the lessons learned on the project.

Planning. Were the plans useful? Did the project team adhere to the plans? Was the quality of the project personnel sufficient? Was the number of personnel in each category sufficient?

Requirements. Were the requirements complete? Were they stable or were there many changes? Were they easy to understand, or were they misinterpreted?

Development. How did the design, coding, and unit testing work out? How did the daily build work? How did software integration work? How did the releases work?

Testing. How did the test planning, test case development, and smoke test development work? How did automated testing work?

New Technology. What impacts did new technology have on costs, schedules, and quality? Did managers and developers interpret these impacts the same way?

Once the material listed in Table 18-1 has been collected and assembled into the Software Project History document, the document should be archived for future use along with the rest of the project materials.

PREPARING THE PROJECT HISTORY CONCLUSIONS FOR USE ON FUTURE PROJECTS

One recurring problem with project histories is that they are completed, archived, and forgotten. To realize maximum benefit from the Software Project History, package the conclusions drawn from the project history analysis in at least these two forms:

◆ Create a planning checklist for future projects. If the project team already has a planning checklist, the checklist should be updated to address the major issues discussed in the project history. This checklist should include both things to do and things to avoid.

◆ Feed the major risks identified during the project into a Top 10 Risks List template, which the next project can use as the basis for its initial risks list.

———◆———

*Converting the project history conclusions into
easily usable forms maximizes the value of the time
and effort the development team puts into creating
the Software Project History and lays a foundation
for the next project to be even more successful.*

———◆———

DISTRIBUTING COPIES OF
THE SOFTWARE PROJECT HISTORY

The completed Software Project History provides a useful supplement to
each team member's individual memory. Holding a printed, bound history
document provides a sense of closure, and each project member should
receive a personal copy.

Survival Check

 The project team creates a written Software Project History that
contains both objective and subjective summary information about
the project.

 The Software Project History isn't created within 15–30 days
of project completion.

 The completed Software Project History is distributed to all project
members.

 The project history conclusions are packaged into a project planning
checklist and an initial risks list for use on the next project.

19
Survival Crib Notes

This book's key guidelines are presented in combination with key guidelines from one of the world's most effective software development organizations: NASA's Software Engineering Laboratory. The end of this chapter provides pointers to additional reading and other resources.

This chapter summarizes the elements needed for software project success by distilling the main messages of this book into a few pages. The first section overviews the approach used by one of NASA's software development organizations. The second describes resources you should consider adding to your personal software survival kit.

NASA's Success Checklist

The Software Engineering Laboratory (SEL) at NASA's Goddard Space Flight Center has been on the cutting edge of software development practices for almost 20 years. It is one of the most competent, most successful software development organizations in the world. In 1994, in recognition of the extraordinary productivity and software quality it had achieved, the SEL became the first organization to win the IEEE's award for software process achievement.

You might think that because NASA's software needs to be ultrareliable, NASA's lessons don't apply to your organization. But think again. The approach that the SEL follows is one that almost any software organization can and should follow. It has enabled the SEL to achieve productivity comparable to the average information systems project and at the same time achieve quality levels that are at least 10 to 20 times better. To put it a little differently, the average information systems shop would need about 14 calendar months and 110 staff months to deliver a 100,000-line-of-code information system, and it would typically contain about 850 defects when delivered. The NASA SEL would deliver a system of that size with about the same amount of time and effort, but it would contain only about 50 defects.

The SEL's *Recommended Approach to Software Development* crystallizes the lessons the SEL has learned over 20 years into a set of nine Dos and eight Don'ts for software project success. These dos and don'ts are presented in the next two sections.

NASA SEL's Dos for Software Success

Here are nine elements of a successful project:

Create and follow a Software Development Plan   At the beginning of the project, prepare a Software Development Plan that describes the project's vision, defines the team structure, and defines the development methods. The plan should include estimates, major milestones, and other measures that will be used to track progress. The Software Development Plan should be a living document that is updated at the end of each major phase or stage.

Empower project personnel   Tap into the project's human potential by aligning the development team members with a project vision, providing the members with a productive environment to work in, and assigning them clear responsibilities and the authority needed to carry out their responsibilities.

Minimize the bureaucracy   Establish the minimum amount of process overhead needed to satisfy the project's objectives. Be sure that there is a good reason for required meetings and paperwork. As NASA says, "More meetings plus more documentation plus more management does not equal more success."

Define the requirements baseline, and manage changes to it   Stabilize requirements as early as possible. Keep a detailed list of potentially volatile requirements or undefined requirements, and prioritize the list by estimated cost and schedule impact. Try to resolve these items during architecture or, at the latest, during detailed design.

Take periodic snapshots of project health and progress, and replan when necessary   Regularly compare the project's progress against the project plan and against similar past projects. If progress deviates significantly from the project plan, replan. Carefully consider reducing the scope of the work when replanning, and try not to be unrealistically optimistic.

Reestimate system size, effort, and schedules periodically   Each new phase of the project provides new information about the software being built. Do not insist on maintaining the original estimates; instead, plan on refining the estimates at the completion of each major milestone. Estimation is an inexact science, and there is nothing wrong with finding that the development team underestimated the project's size or overestimated its own productivity. What is wrong is not planning to periodically check an estimate's accuracy and not correcting the estimate as the project progresses.

Define and manage phase transitions   Some projects lose time in the transition from requirements development to architecture, architecture to stage planning, the end of one stage to the beginning of the next, and so on. The project team should begin preliminary work on the next phase a few weeks before completing the current phase so that the team as a whole can make an efficient transition to the next phase.

Foster a team spirit   Even when a project includes people from different organizations or companies, emphasize the common vision that every person on the project is working toward. Clearly define each person's individual responsibilities, but emphasize the whole-project context within which those responsibilities exist. Be sure to communicate status, risks, and other management issues throughout the project in the same way.

———◆———

No individual is a success who hurts the team, and
no individual is a failure who helps it.

———◆———

Start the project with a small senior staff   Begin the project with a small group of experienced senior people who will provide leadership throughout the project. Be sure they establish a vision, define the software concept, develop an approach to the project, and are generally in alignment with one another before junior staff are brought on board.

NASA SEL's Don'ts for Software Success

Here are eight don'ts for successful projects:

Don't let team members work in an unsystematic way   Efficient development of high quality software is not a touchy-feely, unmanageable process. It is a creative process, but one that benefits from reasoned application of defined principles, practices, methods, and techniques. Insist that the team use systematic development practices.

Don't set unreasonable goals   Setting unreasonable goals is worse than setting no goals at all. If the team doesn't believe in the goals, team members will merely put in their time, punch the clock, and go home. If they are rushed, they will make mistakes upstream that cost fortunes to correct downstream. Set reasonable, moderately challenging goals, and the team will stretch to meet them without damaging project efficiency.

Don't implement changes without assessing their impact and obtaining approval of the change board   Estimate the impact of each change—even important, small changes that the project can absorb without rescheduling. The project needs a record of how it changed over time, both in major and minor ways. Even when a particular change does not have a large impact, small changes add up over time and will eventually cause cost and schedule overruns if not controlled.

Don't gold-plate   Implement only what is required. Developers, managers, and customers often think of small, easy changes that seem to make the software better. But these changes often have much more far-reaching impact than anticipated by the specific developer who implemented the change. Do not let additional complexity creep into the project through gold-plating.

Don't overstaff, especially early in the project   Start the project with a small senior team. Bring additional people onto the project only when there is meaningful work for them to do. This guideline does allow for some early use of junior personnel. During requirements and early architecture, relatively junior staff members can review documents, investigate capabilities of tools and code libraries, and perform many other tasks that require good technical skills but not guru-level standing.

Don't assume that a schedule slip in the middle of a phase will be made up later   One common mistake is to assume that productivity will improve as the project progresses from the beginning of a phase to the end. Productivity might improve slightly, but there isn't enough time within any particular phase to make up time. More generally, do not assume that a schedule slip at any point in the project can be made up later. If the project doesn't catch up soon after a slip is detected, you can safely assume that it won't be possible to catch up.

Don't relax standards in order to cut costs or shorten a schedule   Relaxing standards tends to introduce errors into the project, and optimum project cost and schedule both depend on eliminating errors. Relaxing standards can also have a demotivating effect. Most developers are quality oriented, and a relaxation of standards sends the message that the customer or upper management doesn't care about quality.

Don't assume that a large amount of documentation ensures success   Different projects require different kinds of documentation support. Determine the amount and kind of documentation required based on the project size, schedule, and expected lifetime of the system. Avoid the United States Department of Defense style documentation in which a 25,000-line-of-code program could easily require 5000-10,000 pages of paperwork, and a 100,000-line-of-code program could require as many as 40,000 pages of paperwork.

OTHER SURVIVAL RESOURCES

This book is a software survival guide. You might think of it as the first aid kit you carry in your backpack or car. Just as hospitals are medically better equipped than your trunk, the universe of other software development resources will provide you with many more survival tools than this short guide presents.

BOOKS

Here are some books that have especially good insights mixed with practical advice:

Recommended Approach to Software Development, Revision 3, **Document SEL-81-305, Greenbelt, Maryland: NASA Goddard Space Flight Center, NASA, 1992.** The Software Engineering Laboratory's *Recommended Approach* is probably the most practical overview of running a software project that I have read. It is intended for use specifically with flight dynamics projects, but many of its recommendations are much more broadly applicable. The book describes entry and exit criteria for each project phase and gives cogent summaries of the development team, management team, and various tiger team activities within each phase. The book projects the heartening message that software projects are not mysterious, hard-to-control entities—although they are extremely complex entities, they *can* be controlled through diligent application of lessons learned from previous projects. You can obtain a single copy for free by writing to Software Engineering Branch, Code 552, Goddard Space Flight Center, Greenbelt, Maryland 20771. You can also download the document from the SEL's Web site at *http://fdd.gsfc.nasa.gov/seltext.html.*

Manager's Handbook for Software Development, Revision 1, **Document SEL-84-101, Greenbelt, Maryland: NASA Goddard Space Flight Center, NASA, 1990.** The SEL's *Manager's Handbook* is almost as useful as the *Recommended Approach.* It is shorter, and the guidelines it presents are focused specifically on software project management topics. You can order it or download it in the same way as you can the *Recommended Approach.*

Fergus O'Connell. *How to Run Successful Projects II: The Silver Bullet.* **London, England: Prentice Hall International (UK) Limited, 1996.** O'Connell's book provides a well-written, end-to-end examination of what is needed to run a successful software project. It covers the same ground as the book you're reading now and is quite compatible with it, but there is surprisingly little overlap. Whereas this book provides a big picture technical framework for a project, O'Connell's book focuses on the many specific activities a project manager must perform. It includes many example project forms and planning materials. If, in reading this book, you've asked yourself, "This all sounds good, but what do I *do?*" then O'Connell's book is the right book for you.

Tom Gilb. *Principles of Software Engineering Management.* **Wokingham, England: Addison-Wesley, 1988.** Gilb's book puts the "engineering" into software engineering management by taking a quantitative, risk-oriented approach to conducting a software project. It is based on Gilb's considerable experience as an internationally renowned software project management consultant. This is not the book to read to learn the conventional wisdom about software project success—it takes its own path too often for that. But I think that in many cases in which the book doesn't follow the conventional wisdom, it doesn't because Gilb is right and the conventional wisdom is wrong.

Lawrence H. Putnam and Ware Myers. *Industrial Strength Software: Effective Management Using Measurement*, **Washington, D.C.: IEEE Computer Society Press, 1997.** Putnam and Myers have created an excellent reference that describes how to use software measurement to manage all aspects of software development. In contrast to Gilb's book, Putnam and Myers's book focuses less on specific projects and more on organizational capability. Chapter 21, "Shining Shadow Loses Its Luster," is a special gem— dramatically illustrating the power of quantitative approaches to software project management.

Tom DeMarco and Timothy Lister. *Peopleware: Productive Projects and Teams.* **New York, New York: Dorset House, 1987.** *Peopleware* drives home the message that programming is first and foremost something done by people and only secondarily happens to involve computers. It's entertaining reading, providing memorable stories about software teams that worked and teams that didn't.

Alan M. Davis. *201 Principles of Software Development*, **New York, New York: McGraw-Hill, 1995.** *201 Principles* provides an easy-to-read introduction to the critical issues in software development. Davis's book prepares you to recognize key issues when other books discuss them and when they crop up in your own projects.

Steve McConnell. *Rapid Development.* **Redmond, Washington: Microsoft Press, 1996**   If you've liked this book, you will probably also like what I have to say in *Rapid Development*. It contains general, but still practical, discussions of classic mistakes, risk management, lifecycle planning, scheduling, motivation, teamwork, and many other topics related to rapid software development.

INTERNET RESOURCES

My company has created a *Survival Guide* Web site at *http://www.construx.com/ survivalguide/.* It includes examples of many of the sample documents and forms this book recommends, such as the Software Development Plan, User Interface Style Guide, estimation procedure, Release Sign-off Form, and many more. It also contains links to software development resources on other Web sites, including current links to source-code control tools, time-accounting tools, estimation software, and defect tracking tools. It contains electronic versions of this book's Survival Checks and a spreadsheet version of Chapter 2's Software Project Survival Test.

Epilogue

Bump, bump, bump...

For more than a generation, medium-size projects have been failing for no good reason. They are not advancing software's state of the art. They are not working with cutting-edge research from other fields. They simply topple because they cannot support their own weight. Like Edward Bear, software developers, project managers, and customers bump their heads down the stairs exactly the same way project after project. The course they follow is familiar, but it is inefficient, error-prone, and painful.

Software project survival does not happen accidentally. The work that is required to make a software project succeed is not especially difficult or time-consuming, but it must be executed diligently from the first day of the project to the last.

Software development practice has advanced to a point where few medium-size projects should fail. When developers, managers, and customers stop bumping their heads against the same old problems long enough to acquire the kinds of software project survival skills described in this book, their projects will succeed.

Notes

Preliminary Survival Briefing

Page

vii "About two million people": Data about the number of people working in the software industry comes from Capers Jones, *Applied Software Measurement: Assuring Productivity and Quality, 2d Ed.* New York: McGraw-Hill, 1997. The number of software projects was estimated by combining this data with data on variations in project team sizes from Leland L. Beck and Thomas E. Perkins, "A Survey of Software Engineering Practice: Tools, Methods, and Results," *IEEE Transactions on Software Engineering*, September 1983, pp. 541–61.

vii "Between one-third": This result has been widely reported in sources including Capers Jones, *Patterns of Software Systems Failure and Success*. Boston: International Thomson Computer Press, 1996; The Standish Group, "Charting the Seas of Information Technology," Dennis, MA: The Standish Group, 1994; W. Wayt Gibbs, "Software's Chronic Crisis," *Scientific American*, September 1994, pp. 86-95; Albert L. Lederer and Jayesh Prasad, "Nine Management Guidelines for Better Cost Estimating," *Communications of the ACM*, February 1992, pp. 51–59.

Chapter 1: Welcome to Software Project Survival Training

Page

4 "After detailed plans": Capers Jones, *Assessment and Control of Software Risks*. Englewood Cliffs, NJ: Yourdon Press, 1994.

4 "Abraham Maslow observed": Robert A. Baron, Donn Byrne, and Barry H. Kantowitz, *Psychology: Understanding Behavior, 2d Ed.* New York: Holt, Rinehart and Winston, 1980.

6 "But the project": B. Lakhanpal, "Understanding the Factors Influencing the Performance of Software Development Groups: An Exploratory Group-Level Analysis," *Information and Software Technology*, 35 (8), 1993, pp. 468–73.

7 "I've summarized the rules": Tom Gilb presents a related "Company Communication Bill of Rights" in *Principles of Software Engineering Management*. Wokingham, England: Addison-Wesley, 1988.

Chapter 3: Survival Concepts

Page

26 "Over a 5-year period": Alfred M. Pietrasanta, "A Strategy for Software Process Improvement," Ninth Annual Pacific Northwest Software Quality Conference, October 7–8, 1991, Oregon Convention Center, Portland, OR.

Page

26 "Over a 6.5-year period": Raytheon Electronic Systems, *Advertisement*, *IEEE Software*, September 1995, back cover; Hossein Saiedian and Scott Hamilton, "Case Studies of Hughes and Raytheon's CMM Efforts," *IEEE Computer*, January 1995, pp. 20–21.

26 "Bull HN realized": Herbsleb, James, et al., *Benefits of CMM Based Software Process Improvement: Initial Results*. Pittsburgh: Software Engineering Institute, Document CMU/SEI-94-TR-13, August 1994.

26 "NASA's Software Engineering Laboratory": Victor Basili et al., "SEL's Software Process Improvement Program," *IEEE Software*, November 1995, pp. 83–87.

26 "Similar results have been": Hossein Saiedian and Scott Hamilton, "Case Studies of Hughes and Raytheon's CMM Efforts," *IEEE Computer*, January 1995, pp. 20–21; Lawrence H. Putnam and Ware Myers, *Measures for Excellence: Reliable Software On Time, Within Budget*. Englewood Cliffs, NJ: Yourdon Press, 1992; Myers, Ware, "Good Software Practices Pay Off—Or Do They?" *IEEE Software*, March 1992, pp. 96–97; Herbsleb, James, et al., "Software Process Improvement: State of the Payoff," *American Programmer*, September 1994, pp. 2–12.

26 "It's about a percent": Herbsleb, James, et al., *Benefits of CMM Based Software Process Improvement: Initial Results*. Pittsburgh: Software Engineering Institute, Document CMU/SEI-94-TR-13, August 1994.

27 "In a survey": James Herbsleb, et al., "Software Quality and the Capability Maturity Model," *Communications of the ACM*, June 1997, pp. 30–40. The responses listed were consistent across managers, developers responsible for process improvement, and general senior technical staff members.

29 "Researchers have found": Barry W. Boehm and Philip N. Papaccio, "Understanding and Controlling Software Costs," *IEEE Transactions on Software Engineering*, vol. 14, no. 10, October 1988, pp. 1462–77.

31 "Figure 3-6": The general shape of this figure is based on data from *Manager's Handbook for Software Development, Revision 1*. Document number SEL-84-101. NASA Software Engineering Laboratory, Goddard Space Flight Center, Greenbelt, MD, 1990.

32 "If you want to understand": Laranjeira, Luiz, "Software Size Estimation of Object-Oriented Systems," *IEEE Transactions on Software Engineering*, May 1990.

Chapter 4: Survival Skills

Page

36 "The average project": Harlan D. Mills, *Software Productivity*. Boston, MA: Little, Brown, 1983, pp. 71–81.

36 "A good rule of thumb": Capers Jones, *Assessment and Control of Software Risks*. Englewood Cliffs, NJ: Yourdon Press, 1994.

38 "Planning is so critical": Fergus O'Connell, *How to Run Successful Projects II: The Silver Bullet*. London: Prentice Hall, 1996.

38 "The software industry's experience": Boehm, Barry et al., "Cost Models for Future Software Life Cycle Processes: COCOMO 2.0," *Annals of Software Engineering, Special Volume on Software Process and Product Measurement*, J.D. Arthur and S.M. Henry Eds., Amsterdam: J.C. Baltzer AG, Science Publishers, 1995.

41 "As Tom Gilb says": Tom Gilb, *Principles of Software Engineering Management*. Wokingham, England: Addison-Wesley, 1988.

Page

44 "Or a substantial": Turnover cost for technical employees can be very high. Studies by M. Cherlin and by the Butler Cox Foundation estimate the cost of replacing an experienced computer staff member at anywhere from $20,000 to $100,000 (cited in Rob Thomsett, "Effective Project Teams: A Dilemma, A Model, a Solution," *American Programmer*, July–August 1990, pp. 25–35).

44 "Tom DeMarco and Timothy Lister": Robert A. Zawacki, "Key Issues in Human Resources Management," *Information Systems Management*, Winter 1993, pp. 72–75.

44 "After 15 years": Tom DeMarco and Timothy Lister, *Peopleware: Productive Projects and Teams*. New York: Dorset House, 1987.

45 "The claim in favor": See *Peopleware*, above. Developers who worked in top 25 percent environments were found to be about 2.5 times as productive as developers who worked in bottom 25 percent environments.

45 "For example, studies": Capers Jones points out that, "When considering everything that can be done to improve software productivity, office ergonomics ranks at least as high as other factors such as use of CASE tools, programming language choice, and use of formal processes. In fact, the only technology that outranks office ergonomics is a full-scale software reusability program. (Capers Jones, *Patterns of Software Systems Failure and Success*. Boston: International Thomson Computer Press, 1996.)

47 "In *Usability Engineering*": Jakob Nielsen, *Usability Engineering*. Boston: Academic Press, 1993.

47 "Their review concluded": The Standish Group, "Charting the Seas of Information Technology," Dennis, MA: The Standish Group, 1994.

47 "Experts in rapid": Don Millington and Jennifer Stapleton, "Developing a RAD Standard," *IEEE Software*, September 1995, pp. 54–55.

Chapter 5: The Successful Project at a Glance

Page

52 "Figure 5-1": Adapted from Grady Booch, *Object Solutions: Managing the Object-Oriented Project*. Reading, MA: Addison Wesley, 1996.

60 "Figure 5-4": The figures in this chart are adapted from *Manager's Handbook for Software Development*, Revision 1, SEL-84-101, NASA Software Engineering Laboratory, Goddard Space Flight Center, Greenbelt, MD, November 1990.

61 "Figure 5-5": The figures in this chart are adapted from *Manager's Handbook for Software Development*, Revision 1, SEL-84-101, NASA Software Engineering Laboratory, Goddard Space Flight Center, Greenbelt, MD, November 1990.

62 "Figure 5-6": This code growth graph is adapted from *Manager's Handbook for Software Development*, Revision 1, SEL-84-101, NASA Software Engineering Laboratory, Goddard Space Flight Center, Greenbelt, MD, November 1990.

64 "Figure 5-7": The planning percentages in this figure come from *Manager's Handbook for Software Development*, Revision 1, SEL-84-101, NASA Software Engineering Laboratory, Goddard Space Flight Center, Greenbelt, MD, November 1990. They also involve some expert judgment and will vary somewhat depending on the size of the project and other factors.

Chapter 6: Hitting a Moving Target

Page

74 "As Gene Forte says": Gene Forte, "Managing Change for Rapid Development," *IEEE Software*, March/April 1997, pp. 120–22.

Chapter 7: Preliminary Planning

Page

86 "A study of 75 teams": Carl E. Larson and Frank M. J. LaFasto, *Teamwork: What Must Go Right; What Can Go Wrong*. Newbury Park, CA: Sage, 1989.

87 "Sales and marketing": Steve McConnell, *Rapid Development*. Redmond, WA: Microsoft Press, 1996.

87 "That product ultimately": Marco Iansiti, "Microsoft Corporation: Office Business Unit," Harvard Business School Case Study 9-691-033, Revised May 31, 1994, Boston: Harvard Business School, 1994.

88 "Many surveys have": Rob Thomsett, "Project Pathology: A Study of Project Failures," *American Programmer*, July 1995, pp. 8-16. The Standish Group, 1994. "Charting the Seas of Information Technology," Dennis, MA: The Standish Group, 1994.

90 "One of the most": *Manager's Handbook for Software Development, Revision 1*. Document number SEL-84-101. NASA Software Engineering Laboratory, Goddard Space Flight Center, Greenbelt, MD, 1990.

97 "This list can be": Steve McConnell, *Rapid Development*. Redmond, WA: Microsoft Press, 1996.

100 "The risk-management": Boehm, Barry W., ed., 1989, *Software Risk Management*. Washington, DC: IEEE Computer Society Press, 1989.

101 "To support the peopleware": Software Project Manager's Network, http://spmn.com.

101 "That's a tangible loss": Studies by M. Cherlin and by the Butler Cox Foundation estimate the cost of replacing an experienced computer person at anywhere from $20,000 to $100,000 (Rob Thomsett, "Effective Project Teams: A Dilemma, A Model, a Solution," *American Programmer*, July-August 1990, pp. 25–35). Comparing the loss of five developers to a loss of $250,000 is optimistic.

102 "But new people": Frederick P. Brooks, Jr., *The Mythical Man-Month, Anniversary Edition*. Reading, MA: Addison-Wesley, 1995.

102 "One of the most": H. Sackman, W.J. Erikson, and E.E. Grant, "Exploratory Experimental Studies Comparing Online and Offline Programming Performance." *Communications of the ACM*, vol. 11, no. 1, January 1968, pp. 3-11. Bill Curtis, "Substantiating Programmer Variability," *Proceedings of the IEEE*, vol. 69, no. 7, p. 846; Harlan D. Mills, *Software Productivity*. Boston: Little, Brown, 1983, pp. 71–81; Tom DeMarco and Timothy Lister, "Programmer Performance and the Effects of the Workplace," in *Proceedings of the 8th International Conference on Software Engineering*, August 1985, pp. 268–72; Bill Curtis, et al., "Software Psychology: The Need for an Interdisciplinary Program," *Proceedings of the IEEE*, vol. 74, no. 8, August 1986, pp. 1092–1106; David N. Card, "A Software Technology Evaluation Program," *Information And Software Technology*, vol. 29, no. 6, July/August 1987, pp. 291–300; J. Valett and F. E. McGarry, "A Summary of Software Measurement Experiences in the Software Engineering Laboratory," *Journal of Systems and Software*, vol. 9, no. 2, 1989, pp. 137–48.

Page

103 "One of the more": B. Lakhanpal, "Understanding the Factors Influencing the Performance of Software Development Groups: An Exploratory Group-Level Analysis," *Information and Software Technology*, 35 (8), 1993, pp. 468–73.

103 "Once the project": Carl E. Larson and Frank M. J. LaFasto, *Teamwork: What Must Go Right; What Can Go Wrong*. Newbury Park, CA: Sage, 1989. This study was not specifically about software project personnel, but the conclusions are applicable to software projects.

Chapter 8: Requirements Development

Page

115 "Here are the general": An excellent source of detailed, practical, readable information on designing software for usability is Jakob Nielsen's *Usability Engineering* (Boston: Academic Press, 1993).

Chapter 9: Quality Assurance

Page

126 "Leading-edge companies": Michael Cusumano and Richard Selby, *Microsoft Secrets: How the World's Most Powerful Software Company Creates Technology, Shapes Markets, and Manages People*. New York: Free Press, 1995.

126 "You might think": Richard A. Thomas, "Using Comments to Aid Program Maintenance," *Byte*, May 1984, pp. 415–22.

128 "Anecdotal evidence suggests": See, for example, Steve Maguire, *Writing Solid Code*. Redmond, WA: Microsoft Press, 1993.

131 "Reviews also provide": For more on reviews and inspections, see Tom Gilb and Dorothy Graham, *Software Inspection*. Wokingham, England: Addison-Wesley, 1993; or Daniel P. Freedman and Gerald M. Weinberg, *Handbook of Walkthroughs, Inspections and Technical Reviews, 3d Ed.* New York: Dorset House, 1990.

134 "This is the ratio": Michael Cusumano and Richard Selby, *Microsoft Secrets: How the World's Most Powerful Software Company Creates Technology, Shapes Markets, and Manages People*. New York: Free Press, 1995.

134 "The flight control": Victor Basili and Frank McGarry. "The Experience Factory: How to Build and Run One," Tutorial M1, 17th International Conference on Software Engineering, Seattle, WA, April 24, 1995.

137 "If you want": For suggestions on conducting this kind of supervision, see Jakob Nielsen's *Usability Engineering* (Boston: Academic Press, 1993) or Larry L. Constantine, *Constantine on Peopleware* (Englewood Cliffs, NJ: Yourdon Press, 1995).

138 "Once the software": Who should run the beta test program? If the beta test program is performed for quality assurance purposes, such as compatibility testing, it should be run by the quality assurance group. If the beta test program is performed for any other reason, it should be funded and operated by marketing or whatever other group is interested in the marketing information, improved relationships with clients, or other effects it will produce.

Chapter 10: Architecture

Page

144 "Defining distinct roles": Frederick P. Brooks, Jr., *The Mythical Man-Month, Anniversary Edition*. Reading, MA: Addison-Wesley, 1995.

145 "A good architecture should": For one method of quantitatively assessing how well an architecture fits its problem, see Tom Gilb, "Impact Estimation Tables" (title approximate) in *IEEE Software*, September/October, 1997.

146 "As one measure of": Grady Booch, *Object Solutions: Managing the Object-Oriented Project*. Reading, MA: Addison-Wesley, 1996.

146 "The central thesis of": Frederick P. Brooks, Jr., *The Mythical Man-Month, Anniversary Edition*. Reading, MA: Addison-Wesley, 1995.

148 "For large projects": For more on the Unified Modeling Language (UML), see Rational Software Corporation's Web site at *http://www.rational.com*.

Chapter 11: Final Preparations

Page

164 "A good way to decide": Ken Whitaker, *Managing Software Maniacs*. New York: John Wiley & Sons, 1994.

Chapter 12: Beginning-of-Stage Planning

Page

174 "Members of the software": Software development involves *diseconomies* of scale. The larger the project, the more interrelationships exist among different software components, and the more complicated and difficult software development becomes. Because complexity increases multiplicatively, and effort is related to complexity, the amount of effort needed to develop a program increases faster than program size does. A 25,000-line-of-code shrink-wrap program would typically require about 20 staff months of development effort. Increasing the system size by a factor of three, to 75,000 lines of code, would increase the amount of effort required by about a factor of seven, to about 140 staff months. Because of this phenomenon, developing three 25,000-line-of-code programs instead of one 75,000-line-of-code program is the most economical alternative. In practice, breaking a 75,000-line-of-code program into three stages won't produce savings as dramatic as if the stages were three distinct programs, but you can still use the general effect to your project's benefit.

180 "The most common source": Michiel van Genuchten, "Why is Software Late? An Empirical Study of Reasons for Delay in Software Development," *IEEE Transactions on Software Engineering*, vol. 17, no. 6, June 1991, pp. 582–90.

183 "As Barry Boehm": Barry Boehm and Rony Ross, "Theory-W Software Project Management: Principles and Examples," *IEEE Transactions on Software Engineering*, 15 (7) July 1989, pp. 902–16.

184 "If the miniature milestone plan": Fergus O'Connell, *How to Run Successful Projects II: The Silver Bullet*. London: Prentice Hall International (UK) Limited, 1996.

Page

Chapter 13: Detailed Design

Page

192 "Numerous software engineering studies": A study at NASA's Software Engineering Laboratory found that only 29 percent of the errors found by code reading were detected by both of two code readers (Ara Kouchakdjian, Scott Green, and Victor Basili, "Evaluation of the Cleanroom Methodology in the Software Engineering Laboratory," *Proceedings of the Fourteenth Annual Software Engineering Workshop, November 29, 1989,* Greenbelt, MD: Goddard Space Flight Center, Document number SEL-89-007). Glenford J. Myers reported similar results in "A Controlled Experiment in Program Testing and Code Walkthroughs/Inspections," *Communications of the ACM,* vol. 21, no. 9, pp. 760–68.

192 "The project will probably": Marilyn Bush and John Kelly found that the number of defects detected did not increase significantly with more than three reviewers, in "The Jet Propulsion Laboratory's Experience with Formal Inspections," *Proceedings of the Fourteenth Annual Software Engineering Workshop, November 29, 1989,* Greenbelt, MD: Goddard Space Flight Center, Document number SEL-89-007.

192 "This pre-meeting review work": Lawrence G. Votta, et al., "Investigating the Application of Capture-Recapture Techniques to Requirements and Design Reviews" *Proceedings of the Sixteenth Annual Software Engineering Workshop, December 4–5, 1991,* Greenbelt, MD: Goddard Space Flight Center, Document number SEL-91-006.

192 "Reviewing much less": Humphrey S. Watts, *Managing the Software Process.* Reading, MA, Addison-Wesley, 1989.

192 "Studies of software maintenance": G. Parikh and N. Zvegintzov, eds., *Tutorial on Software Maintenance.* Los Alamitos, CA: IEEE Computer Society Press, 1983.

193 "Since the average program": Richard A. Thomas, "Using Comments to Aid Program Maintenance," *Byte,* May 1984, pp. 415–22.

194 "That code had been": Bashar Nuseibeh, "Ariane 5: Who Dunnit?" *IEEE Software,* May/June 1997, pp. 15–16.

195 "The savings potential": Tom Gilb, *Principles of Software Engineering Management.* Wokingham, England: Addison-Wesley, 1988.

195 "Because they can be": Tom Gilb and Dorothy Graham. *Software Inspection.* Wokingham, England: Addison-Wesley, 1993.

195 "One study of large": Glen W. Russell, "Experience with Inspection in Ultralarge-Scale Developments," *IEEE Software,* vol. 8, no. 1, January 1991, pp. 25–31.

197 "Most often, the first-stage implementation": Grady Booch, *Object Solutions: Managing the Object-Oriented Project.* Reading, MA: Addison-Wesley, 1996.

Chapter 14: Construction

Page

201 "Maximum length of": In *Code Complete* (Microsoft Press, 1993), I recommend not setting arbitrary limits on the length routines can have. This recommendation was a response to the common practice of setting limits of 50 lines or 2 pages. Coding standards can and should set limits on routine length, but these limits should be fairly high—200 lines or higher. Projects should also set guidelines for the length at which reviewers should pay special attention to whether long routines have been designed and implemented as well as they could be.

Page

208 "Infrastructure development has": The use of requirements traceability matrixes helps with this problem. If each part of the system is required to be traceable back to the requirements, a developer won't be able to slip nonessential functionality into the foundation or at least won't be able to get it past the design review. Nonrequired functionality found during a design review should be removed before proceeding with construction.

Chapter 15: System Testing

Page

218 "This practice helps to": Steve Maguire makes a similar point in *Writing Solid Code.* Redmond, WA: Microsoft Press, 1993.

218 "Commonly, about 80 percent": Barry W. Boehm, "Improving Software Productivity," *IEEE Computer,* September 1987, pp. 43–57; Capers Jones, *Applied Software Measurement: Assuring Productivity and Quality, 2d Ed.* New York: McGraw-Hill, 1997.

Chapter 16: Software Release

Page

224 "Figure 16-1 shows": Adapted from *Software Engineering Laboratory (SEL) Relationships, Models, and Management Rules,* Document number SEL-91-001. NASA Software Engineering Laboratory, Goddard Space Flight Center, Greenbelt, MD, February 1991.

226 "If you want to remove": The idea of releasing software when less than 100 percent of the defects have been removed might be unfamiliar to you. Some project teams think that they have found all the defects in their software just because they bring the open defect count down to 0 before release. This is nearly always a temporary state, and additional defects are found after the software is put into operation. When the consequence of software failure is likely to be a human life, a plan to achieve 0 defects is a realistic and justified goal, but it will increase the cost of the software by a large factor. For example, as mentioned in an earlier note, on the space shuttle software, NASA used 10 testers for each developer. When the consequence of software failure is less serious than a loss of human life, a plan to detect 100 percent of all defects prior to release usually cannot be cost justified.

226 "Another simple defect": Glenford J. Myers, *Software Reliability.* New York: John Wiley, 1976.

227 "They would then capture": Tom Gilb describes this approach as "bebugging" in *Software Metrics.* Cambridge, MA: Winthrop Publishers, 1977.

228 "Almost 400 defects have": The estimates described do not include confidence levels. The confidence level of the estimate is a complex combination of the number of indigenous defects detected, number of seeded defects detected, number of defects seeded, and the acceptable margin of error. In the example, the confidence level is 75 percent that the number of defects is between 774 and 1161. A utility program that computes an estimate's confidence level from these factors is available from the *Survival Guide* Web site.

231 "The Release Checklist for": Dennis Adler, Microsoft Corporation, private communication, March 7, 1997.

Page

232 "Verify that the correct": This list of registry entries would typically exist in a related document and could be attached to the Release Checklist. Platforms other than Windows might not have "registry entries," but they will often have "environment variables" or something similar.

Chapter 17: End-of-Stage Wrap-Up

Page

240 "A 1991 survey of over": Michiel van Genuchten, "Why is Software Late? An Empirical Study of Reasons for Delay in Software Development," *IEEE Transactions on Software Engineering*, vol. 17, no. 6, June 1991, pp. 582–90.

Chapter 18: Project History

Page

249 "Some projects have had": Matthew J. Slattery, private communication, May 12, 1997.

249 "The combination of quantitative": This project history was inspired in substantial part by the "Software Development History" contained in *Recommended Approach to Software Development, Revision 3*. Document number SEL-81-305. NASA Software Engineering Laboratory, Goddard Space Flight Center, Greenbelt, MD, 1992.

251 "Feed the major risks": Bonnie Collier, Tom DeMarco, and Peter Fearey, "A Defined Process for Project Postmortem Review," *IEEE Software*, July 1996, pp. 65–71.

Chapter 19: Survival Crib Notes

Page

254 "The NASA SEL would deliver": Data on error rate for MIS systems comes from Capers Jones, *Applied Software Measurement, 2d Ed*. New York: McGraw-Hill, 1997. Data on NASA SEL error rate comes from *Software Engineering Laboratory (SEL) Relationships, Models, and Management Rules*. Document number SEL-91-001. NASA Software Engineering Laboratory, Goddard Space Flight Center, Greenbelt, MD, February 1991.

254 "They are presented here": *Recommended Approach to Software Development, Revision 3*, Document number SEL-81-305. NASA Software Engineering Laboratory, Goddard Space Flight Center, Greenbelt, MD, June 1992.

257 "Avoid the United States": These paperwork figures are based on data in Capers Jones, *Applied Software Measurement: Assuring Productivity and Quality, 2d Ed*. New York: McGraw-Hill, 1997.

GLOSSARY

ACM. Acronym for Association of Computing Machinery, a professional membership organization that provides a variety of member services to people who work with computers.

Analysis. See *Requirements analysis*.

Applications programs. The kind of software developed for use by end users. Examples of applications include spreadsheet, word-processing, and accounting programs. Compare *Information systems, Real-time software, Shrink-wrap software*, and *Systems software*.

Architecture. The design of the organizational structure of a system, its communications rules, and systemwide design and implementation guidelines. Architecture is also sometimes referred to as "system architecture," "design," "high-level design," and "top-level design." The term "architecture" can also refer to the architecture document.

Baseline, *n.* The original version of a work product that serves as the basis for all future development work, that is placed under change control, and that can be changed only through the systematic change control process.

Baseline, *v.* To place a work product under change control for the first time.

Build. A specific instance of a software program at a particular time during its development. Builds are often numbered. At the end of the project, a specific build will be released or accepted. Compare *Delivery* and *Release*.

Build instructions.   See *Software build instructions*.

Change board.   The group of people responsible for evaluating Change Proposals, approving or rejecting them, and notifying affected parties of how each one was resolved.

Change Control Plan.   The document that describes how change control will be conducted on a specific project.

Change control.   The practice of managing changes in requirements, architecture, design, source code, and other work products.

Change Proposal.   A document or form used to propose changes as part of a systematic change control process. A Change Proposal typically includes a description of the change; an evaluation of impacts that the change will have on cost, schedule, quality, and other product and project characteristics; and a justification of why the change is needed.

Code reading.   A code review technique in which source code is read by one or more programmers before a review meeting is held. Compare *Code review, Inspection,* and *Walkthrough*.

Code review.   A technical review that focuses on a system's source code. See *Technical review*.

Coding Standard.   A document describing the detailed conventions that developers must follow in creating a system's source code.

Coding.   See *Construction*.

Complexity.   The degree to which a system's design or code is difficult to understand because of numerous components or relationships among components.

Cone of uncertainty.   The amount of possible error in a software project estimate, which is very large in the early stages of a project and shrinks dramatically as the project nears completion.

Construction.   The activity in software development comprising detailed design, coding, unit testing, and debugging. This activity is also commonly known as "coding," "implementation," and "programming."

Control.   The ability to direct the outcome of a project's cost, schedule, functionality, or other characteristics. Compare *Visibility*.

Customer. The person or persons that the software ultimately must please in order to be considered a success. For information systems, often the customer is an in-house end user. For shrink-wrap software, the customer is a person or organization that buys the software. For custom software, the customer is the organization that contracts with the software development organization in order to develop a system.

Daily build and smoke test. A development practice in which a version of the software is built every day and then subjected to a short test to determine whether it "smokes" (breaks). If the build is found to be stable enough for the test group to work with, the build passes the smoke test.

Defect. An error in a program's specification, design, or implementation.

Defect tracking. The practice of recording all defects found in the executable software and other work products and monitoring them throughout the project.

Deliverable. Any work product that must be delivered to someone other than the work product's author.

Delivery. The release of software to users outside the group that is responsible for the development of the software. Software can be delivered by developers to a testing group, internal users, or external customers. "Delivery" and "release" are used interchangeably. Compare *Build* and *Release*.

Deployment Document (Cutover Handbook). The document that describes how to put a new system into operation, especially what must be done for a new system to replace an older system.

Design. The process of conceiving, inventing, or contriving a scheme for turning a specification for a computer program into an operational program; the activity that links requirements development to construction. "Design" also refers to the result of the design activity. Compare *Architecture* and *Detailed design*.

Design review. A technical review that focuses on a system's design. Compare *Technical review*.

Detailed design. Software design work that focuses on operations of individual routines and small collections of routines. Compare *Architecture*.

Detailed Design Document. A document that describes the detailed design for a specific part of a system. See *Detailed design.*

Downstream. Usually refers to construction and system testing, but can also refer to any part of a software project that follows any other particular part. Compare *Upstream.*

End user. The ultimate user of a program. The end user of a word processing program could be an administrative assistant or a writer. The end user of a compiler could be a software developer. Compare *Customer.*

End-user documentation. Books, reference cards, help screens, and other materials that are delivered to end users.

Go/no go decision. A decision made during the project's Planning Checkpoint Review about whether to continue a project.

High level. General, broad, and abstract, as in "high-level design" or "high-level milestones." Compare *Top level.*

High-level design. Software design activity that is more like architecture than detailed design. Compare *Architecture* and *Detailed design.*

IEEE. Acronym for Institute of Electrical and Electronics Engineers, a professional membership organization that provides a variety of member services to software developers and other kinds of engineers.

Implementation. Essentially the same as construction. Also refers to the work products created during construction, such as source code. See *Construction.*

Individual Stage Plan. The document that contains a detailed plan, which includes miniature milestones, for performing work during a single stage of a project using staged delivery.

Information systems (IS). The kind of software developed for use in general business operations, such as payroll software, accounting software, and billing software. Compare *Applications programs, Real-time software, Shrink-wrap software,* and *Systems software.*

Inspection. A technical review technique characterized by use of individual code reading, checklists to focus each reviewer's attention, review meetings that inspect each line of code interactively, and systematic feedback from the review process to improve future reviews.

Install program. A specific kind of program that is run to set up new software on a computer.

Integration. The activity of combining multiple software components and making them work together.

Integration testing. The testing of software components that have been integrated.

Line of code. A programming language statement, often defined as a noncomment, nonblank source statement.

Low level. Specific, detailed, and concrete, as in "low-level design" or "low-level milestones."

Make files. See *Software build instructions (make files)*.

Maintainability. The ease with which a software system can be modified to change or add capabilities, improve performance, or correct defects.

Miniature milestone. A task that takes a few days or less to perform, and for project tracking purposes, is considered to be either done or not done, but never partially done. Miniature milestones are also called "inch pebbles" and "microstones."

Object-oriented design. An approach to software design that makes use of object-oriented programming concepts.

Object-oriented programming. A kind of computer programming that focuses on building computer programs from collections of objects (amalgamations of data and operations on data that are treated as unified entities). Programming languages that support object-oriented programming include C++, Java, and Smalltalk.

People-aware management accountability. The practice of holding managers accountable for the condition of the human resources on their projects, especially for whether people emerge from their projects worth more or less to their organizations.

Phase. A period during which a project team focuses primarily on a specific kind of work, such as the requirements development, architecture, construction, and release phases. Compare *Stage*.

Planning Checkpoint Review. A review held about 10 to 20 percent of the way through a software project to determine whether the project planning, requirements development, and initial architecture work is sufficient to support development of the rest of the software. A go/no go decision is made during this review.

Postmortem.   A phase at the end of a software project during which project team members evaluate the project and learn lessons that can be applied to the next project. "Postmortem" also refers to the report created during the postmortem phase.

Programming.   The general activity of software development, especially construction activities. Compare *Construction*.

Project tracking.   Monitoring the status of a project by regularly comparing actual results to planned results, such as comparing the actual schedule and budget to the planned schedule and budget, or the actual functionality present to the required functionality.

Prototype, *n.*   See *User Interface Prototype*.

Prototype, *v.*   A development technique in which a preliminary version of a program or subprogram is developed to facilitate user feedback or examine other development issues.

Pseudocode.   English-like statements that are used for low-level program design.

Quality assurance (QA).   A planned and systematic pattern of activities designed to ensure that a system has the desired characteristics.

Quality Assurance Plan.   The document that describes the specific quality assurance practices a software project intends to use.

Readability.   The ease with which a person can read and understand the source code of a system, especially at the detailed statement level.

Real-time software.   The kind of software that deals with systems that must operate within a time frame determined by external constraints. Typical real-time systems include avionics and manufacturing control programs. Compare *Applications programs, Information systems, Shrink-wrap software,* and *Systems software*.

Release.   The delivery of software to users who are outside the group that is responsible for the development of the software. Software can be released by developers to a testing group, to internal users, or to external customers. "Release" and "delivery" are used interchangeably. Compare *Acceptance, Build,* and *Delivery*.

Release Checklist.   A form containing a list of activities that should be performed during the release phase of a project to prevent software that is not ready to be released from being released.

Release Sign-off Form.   A form that project stakeholders sign to record their agreement that a software program is ready to be released to the customer.

Requirements.   A detailed description of what the software is supposed to do. Compare *Requirements development* and *User Manual/Requirements Specification*.

Requirements analysis.   See *Requirements development*.

Requirements development.   The software development phase during which user needs are explored and both the users and the development team acquire a detailed understanding of what software should be created.

Requirements specification.   1. The document that contains statements of requirements. 2. The activity of committing requirements to writing. 3. The phase during which requirements are explored and developed. See *Requirements development*.

Requirements traceability.   The ability to determine for each requirement which parts of the system's architecture, design, and implementation were created to satisfy that requirement and vice versa.

Reusability.   The extent to and ease with which parts of a system can be put to use in other systems.

Review.   See *Technical review*.

Revision control.   Archival and retrieval of specific work products, usually stored in electronic form, through an automated system. Compare *Change control* and *Source-code control*.

Risk.   An undesirable outcome.

Shrink-wrap software.   The kind of software developed for the mass market and sold in retail stores, such as word processors, spreadsheets, and project planners. Compare *Applications programs, Information systems, Real-time software,* and *Systems software*.

Smoke test.   See *Daily build and smoke test*.

Software Architecture Document.   The document that describes a program's architectural design. Compare *Architecture*.

Software build instructions (make files). The scripts and other instructions that software developers use to automate the process of converting source code into executable software.

Software Construction Plan. A plan that describes how a specific software component will be created, including miniature milestones.

Software Development Plan. The document that describes how a software project will be conducted. The project plan includes schedules, budgets, estimates, and technical methodologies; it is updated to include detailed plans for each phase throughout the project.

Software Integration Procedure. The sequence of steps that developers must follow when they combine newly developed code with code that has already been integrated.

Software Project History document. The document that summarizes the course of the project and the lessons learned by the project team during the project. Also called the Software Project History.

Software Project Log. A record book or document in which project characteristics are regularly recorded, including staff hours, defect counts, lines of code, and so on.

Software release. See *Release*.

Software test case. See *Test case*.

Source code control. The specific kind of revision control used to control source code. See *Revision control*.

Source code tracing. The activity of stepping through source code line by line in a symbolic debugger for the purpose of watching the program flow, observing changes in variables, and determining whether the source code operates as intended.

Source code. The detailed, human readable instructions that directly or indirectly describe to the computer how a software system should operate.

Specification. Synonym for "requirements." Occasionally refers to architecture, but that use is nonstandard.

Stage. A period during a staged delivery project that includes the activities of detailed design, construction, test, and delivery. A stage is essentially a project in miniature. Compare *Phase*.

Staged delivery cycle. See *Stage*.

Staged Delivery Plan. A plan that specifies during which stage of a staged delivery project each detailed requirement will be delivered.

Staged delivery project. A project that performs requirements development and architecture for a whole system, then delivers the software in multiple stages, driving the software to a quality level at the end of each stage sufficient to release the software to end users, if desired.

Staged delivery. A delivery made at the end of a stage. Compare *Delivery* and *Stage*.

System. Generally, a whole program. Sometimes used more specifically to refer to operating-system level code.

System test. Systematic exercise of an entire program for the purpose of finding defects.

Systems software. The kind of software for use by the computer itself or by software developers, including operating systems, device drivers, compilers, and so on. Compare *Applications programs, Information systems, Real-time software,* and *Shrink-wrap software.*

Technical review. A catchall term for inspections, walkthroughs, code reading, and other practices in which one or more persons examines the work of another person for the purpose of improving its quality.

Test. Execution of a program for the purpose of finding defects.

Test case. A description of inputs, execution instructions, and expected results, which are created for the purpose of determining whether a specific software feature works correctly or a specific requirement has been satisfied.

Top 10 Risks List. A document that describes the most significant risks to a project in priority order and that is updated about twice a month.

Top level. The most general, broad, and abstract, as in "top-level design" or "top-level milestones." Compare *High level*.

Tracking. See *Project tracking*.

Understandability. The ease with which a system can be comprehended at both the system organizational and detailed statement levels. Understandability has to do with the coherence of the system at a more general level than readability. Compare *Readability*.

Unified Modeling Language (UML). A diagrammatic convention for expressing the kind of software design that is known as object-oriented design.

Unit test. Execution of individual routines and modules by the developer or by an independent tester for the purpose of finding defects.

Upstream. Usually refers to requirements development and architecture, but can also refer to any part of a software project that precedes any other particular part. Compare *Downstream*.

User interface. The visible part of a program including menus, dialog boxes, and other on-screen elements.

User Interface Prototype. A mock-up of software under development that is created for the purpose of eliciting user feedback about the software's intended functionality and look and feel.

User Interface Style Guide. A document that specifies the way that the software should look and feel and guides detailed user-interface development.

User Manual/Requirements Specification. A document created during the requirements development phase that is used both as end-user documentation and as a specification of the software's requirements.

Visibility. The ease and accuracy with which it is possible to assess the status of a project's cost, schedule, functionality, or other characteristics. Compare *Control*.

Vision statement. A description of the highest level objective of the project.

Walkthrough. A relatively informal review technique in which a developer leads members of a review team through a design or code and the review team identifies possible problems and improvements.

Work product. The tangible result of work performed. Examples of work products include executable software, documents, and test cases.

Index

Page numbers in italics refer to tables, figures, or illustrations.

A

B

C

About the Author

Steve McConnell is Chief Software Engineer at Construx Software Builders, where he divides his time between leading custom software projects, consulting on other companies' software projects, and writing books and articles. He is the author of *Code Complete* (1993) and *Rapid Development* (1996), both winners of *Software Development* magazine's Jolt award for outstanding software development books. Steve has also written numerous technical articles, and edits *IEEE Software* magazine's "Best Practices" column.

Steve earned a Bachelor's degree from Whitman College in Walla Walla, Washington and a Master's degree in software engineering from Seattle University. He is an editorial board member of *IEEE Software* and *Software Practitioner*, a senior reviewer for *IEEE Computer* magazine, and a member of the IEEE Computer Society and ACM.

Steve lives in Bellevue, Washington with his wife, Tammy, and two dogs, Odie and Daisy.

If you have any comments or questions about this book, please contact Steve by mail care of Microsoft Press, on the Internet at stevemcc@construx.com, or at Steve's Web site, *http://www.construx.com/stevemcc/*.

SURVIVAL GUIDE WEB SITE

`http://www.construx.com/survivalguide/`

This book has a companion Web site, *http://www.construx.com/survivalguide/*, which is referred to throughout as the *Survival Guide* Web site. The Web site contains many materials related to the contents of the book, including electronic versions of the Software Project Survival Test in Chapter 2; the project plan in Chapter 5; all of this book's Survival Checks; free Construx Estimate project estimation software; sample forms, such as Release Checklists, defect reports, Change Proposals, and Software Project Logs; checklists for use throughout a software project; and links to current versions of the productivity tools described throughout the book, including version control, time accounting, defect tracking, user-interface prototyping, and other products.

———◆———

The manuscript for this book was prepared using Microsoft Word 97. Pages were composed by Microsoft Press, with text and display type in Palatino. Composed pages were delivered to the printer as electronic prepress files.

Cover Designer
Greg Hickman

Principal Artist
Michael Victor

Cover Illustrator
Todd Daman

Compositors
Abby Hall, Steven Hopster

Interior Graphic Designer
Kim M. Eggleston

Indexer
Julie Kawabata

Register Today!

Return this
Software Project Survival Guide
registration card for
a Microsoft Press® catalog

U.S. and Canada addresses only. Fill in information below and mail postage-free. Please mail only the bottom half of this page.

1-57231-621-7A   *SOFTWARE PROJECT SURVIVAL GUIDE*   *Owner Registration Card*

_____

NAME

_____

INSTITUTION OR COMPANY NAME

_____

ADDRESS

_____

_____

CITY   STATE   ZIP

Microsoft® Press
Quality Computer Books

**For a free catalog of
Microsoft Press® products, call
1-800-MSPRESS**

NO POSTAGE
NECESSARY
IF MAILED
IN THE
UNITED STATES

BUSINESS REPLY MAIL
FIRST-CLASS MAIL   PERMIT NO. 53   BOTHELL, WA

POSTAGE WILL BE PAID BY ADDRESSEE

MICROSOFT PRESS REGISTRATION
SOFTWARE PROJECT SURVIVAL GUIDE
PO BOX 3019
BOTHELL   WA   98041-9946

3702652326

X

**PARK
LEARNING CENTRE**

The Park, Cheltenham
Gloucestershire GL50 2QF
Telephone: 01242 532721

UNIVERSITY OF
GLOUCESTERSHIRE·

WEEK LOAN

WEEK LOAN

1 4 DEC 2000
2 4 OCT 2003
- 8 MAR 2001
- 2 JUN 2004
- 4 MAY 2001
8 JUN 2004
- 6 DEC 2001
1 4 JAN 2005
1 8 JAN 2002
1 6 MAY 2005
- 5 JUN 2002
2 5 NOV 2002
1 7 NOV 2006
1 9 JAN 2007
1 2 MAR 2003
- 6 JUN 2003

WITHDRAWN